Halfway Down the Hall

Wesleyan Poetry

HALFWAY
DOWN
THE
HALL

New and Selected Poems

Rachel Hadas

Wesleyan University Press
Published by University Press of New England
Hanover and London

Wesleyan University Press

Published by University Press of New England, Hanover, NH 03755

This collection © 1998 by Rachel Hadas
Printed in the United States of America

5 4 3 2 1

CIP data appear at the end of the book

This gathering of the work of many years

is lovingly dedicated

to George, Jonathan, and Beth—

my husband, my son, and my sister.

Contents

from **Pass It On** (1989)

from **Living in Time** (1990)

from **Unending Dialogue** (1991)

Acknowledgments

Some of the poems in this collection have previously appeared in periodicals, sometimes under different titles or in slightly different versions. These include: *Aegean Review*, "Last Trip to Greece"; *Agni Review*, "The End of Summer"; *American Scholar*, "Elegy Variations Part I"; *Arion*, "Tibullus I.ii"; *Atlanta Review*, "The Slip," "The Myth of a Happy Childhood"; *Boston Review*, "Rag Rug"; *Boulevard*, "First Night Back," "Nourishment"; *Canto*, "Making Sense of Salt Water," "Five Disguises"; *Central Park*, "Alien Corn"; *Crosscurrents*, "Moments of Summer"; *Cumberland Poetry Review*, "The Oyster Grain"; *Denver Quarterly*, "Along Edges," "Triptych," "Teaching the Iliad," "Less Than Kind," "On Poetry"; *Epoch*, "Codex Minor"; *The Formalist*, "Auguries," "Benefit Night, New York City Ballet"; *Harvard Magazine*, "Alternatives"; *Kenyon Review*, "Recoveries"; *Margin*, "Generations"; *The New Criterion*, "Fleshly Answers," "Idolatry Brood," "On That Mountain"; *The New Republic*, "Shells," "The Poles," "Little by Little," "Fin de Siècle," "The Last Movie"; *New York Review of Books*, "The Voice"; *The New Yorker*, "Still Life in Garden," "Riverside Park," "A Gust," "The Red Hat," "Falcon," "Wish Granted," "Four Lives, Stirring," "The Red House"; *PN Review*, "Aurora," "Song"; *Paris Review*, "Searching the Scriptures," "The Hinge"; *Partisan Review*. "The Peacock in the Garden," "Greek Gold," "Pass It On, III"; *Pequod*, "The Swan"; *Poetry*, "Twelfth Birthday"; *Prairie Schooner*, "Hortus Conclusus"; *The Progressive*, "Stress"; *Raritan*, "At *The Tempest*," "Lullaby"; *Shenandoah*, "Three Silences"; *Southwest Review*, "Pomology", "Two and One," "Pass It On, I," "Learning to Talk," "Spring," "Mars and Venus"; *Tennessee Quarterly*, "Voyage to Cythera," "Pomegranates"; *Three Penny Review*, "Mayday at the Frick," "Mom and Dad," "Mutability," "The Revenant," "In the Middle," "Upon My Mother's Death"; *Times Literary Supplement*, "Flying Home"; *Verse*, "Genealogies"; *Western Humanities Review*, "Performances, Assortments," "City and Country," "Peculiar Sanctity"; *Yale Review*, "Myth (ii)." "Black Light," "Roadblock," "Arguments of Silence."

New Poems

RAG RUG

It has arrived at last—the long rag rug
   multiply folded. On top, one alien hair.
      I put my face to the folds and smell despair
        palpable as salt air
      in all those rooms and houses, small and smug—
enclosures I passed through on my way where?

Whoever did the weaving appears old
   in my mind's eye. I can't make out her face,
      can only conjure up the faintest trace
        of an abstracted grace,
      clack of the loom. Does she know they'll be sold,
these precious things, in some unheard-of place?

I perch her on a hill, precariously
   beyond the reach of the waves' daily boom.
      Sun blazes overhead, but her dim room
        (no bigger than the loom)
      is proof against the violence of the sky.
From it I further spin what I once called my home:

Endless horizons fading into haze,
   the mornings dawn came up so rosy-clear;
      snails in the garden, sheep bells everywhere,
        the brightness of the air,
      terraces, valleys organizing space
and time's cessation. So this package here

I'm now unwrapping, in New York, today
   (rugs like rainbows, woven with a grace
      my strands of language barely can express;
        dishrags of dailiness
      dispersed and recombined and freshly gay)
comes to me imbued with images,

slowly and faithfully across the water,
  across the world. It represents a time
    I myself snipped and recombined as rhyme
      as soon as I went home,
    if that is where I am. These rugs recover
the sense of stepping twice into a single river.

LAST TRIP TO GREECE

I had the labels ready with their essence:
Add water, serve. Light, language, beauty, sea,
body, etcetera, etcetera. Time.
In honesty I need to change the tune:
queasiness, boredom, and misogyny.
Forget the little table by the sea
under an awning. Stupefied by sun,
we were to have sat musing over dreams
dreamed in the shuttered twilight of siestas.
No. There was sitting, though—sitting and waiting.
Minutes ticked by. The sluggish month of June
little by little shifted its big bulk,
morning to evening, dawn to afternoon,
till it was time to climb back on the plane.

The very language was to have been a spell
I'd left half woven, alien, magical,
testing the murky waters with my tongue . . .
Ha! I remembered everything too well.
Words meant the culture that they dragged along.
I entered it each time I acquiesced
to vowels and consonants and all the rest.
The language had three genders, it was true,
but only one that mattered. What was new
was how I saw this world as one of men.
The energy was men's, men's was the joy:
the sun-dark muscles at the soccer match
matched the colossal kouros' marble thigh,
the only thing of beauty in Vathy—

skillfully rendered, lovingly observed,
alert and timeless in its stony way.
But these were partial pleasures—half a world.
Where was the realm of women? Where was I?
Could all we weaker vessels be boiled down
to that one expedition to the convent?
We rose so early sun and moon still shared the sky
to climb the mountain, find the nuns halfway
to heaven, but beyond the reach of time,
of energy clocked by sinew or by speed.
With their cracked bells, devotions, goats, and hens,
their sanctuary of bees and running water,
their milk and ouzo offered thirsty travelers,
do they have all of paradise they need?

I wasn't made to live in paradise.
And I'd this misconception about time.
The precious element became a baggy
garment in whose folds I nearly smothered,
however fervently I'd dreamed of it
before I put it on. For too much time
is like a swirling cloak without an opening.
You cannot use your arms to work, you almost
go down like Agamemnon in the bath
speared by his furious consort Clytemnestra,
that queen whose weapon bridged two worlds with blood—
and whom, although I thought I knew the myth,
I grew to be more sympathetic with.
Oh, everything had changed! Or was it simply me?

Idées reçues I'd readily affixed
to nature like a pair of rosy lenses
had somehow come undone. The gentle sheep bells
tinkling on Acrocorinth when I first
visited the place ten years ago
still tintinnabulated; but this time
what made the day was an enormous snake
sliding into a hole. He owned the place.
He—but why he? What sex are guardian serpents?
And who was I? Well, newly pregnant; queasy;
uneasy in the combat zone I kept
perceiving between what were now two worlds,
the fight a sudden struggle in my gut.
Oh god, how much I wanted to go home!

Urgency was the measure of regret
for what I'd had and seen and lost and learned;
of hope, as well, for what I was becoming,
for what I needed distance to make true.
Dreams meanwhile took on firm geometries:
one family member wedged into each corner,
the loaded silence palpable between them
as I took courage, made my brief announcement,
and shattered certain symmetries for good.
Forever. Change on both sides, in the middle;
change in my middle. I wasn't pedestaled,
entranced in a museum; nor did I float
dreamily above the pool of time.
All the old lineaments were ripe for change.

THE SLIP

Empty and trembling, haloed by absences,
whooshings, invisible leave-takings, finishes,
images, closure: departures so gracefully
practice their gestures that when they do happen,
dazzled with sunlight, distracted by darkness,
mercifully often we miss the event.
So many hours, days, weeks, years, and decades
spent—no, slathered and lavished and squandered
ardently, avidly gazing at nothing,
pacing the pavement or peering round corners,
setting the table and sniffing the twilight,
sitting and gazing at edges, horizons,
preparing occasions that leave us exhausted,
recovering, staggering back to a climax.
Dramas of use, inanition, repletion!
And there all along, except not there forever,
was the beloved. The foreground? The background?
Thoughtful, impatient, affectionate, angry,
tired, distracted, preoccupied, human,
part of our lives past quotidian limits,
there all the while and yet not there forever.

STILL LIFE IN GARDEN

Speechless, considering, feet well apart:
exactly how my mother would take root
deep in the garden, so you stand. It's early;
a summer day spreads out.
Bushier by the hour, long wavering rows
form lines and paths and furrows as of thought
marking a brow.
It's a small garden; no
reason for amazement if you tread
neatly in the footsteps of the dead.
Stealthily day by day
tomatoes, beans, cucumbers take on gloss
and heft, and everything seems effortless,
except the digging, planting, weeding—plus
the same vague tenderness,
the deep and inexhaustible green brood
you now are lost in, standing where she stood.

POMOLOGY

Sappho, of the numberless kinds of apples
we have two, and one of them ripens early,
striped with sweetness, fragrant and lambent, by mid-
           August already

falling even on utterly windless days in-
to high grasses, ditches, to lie, wet, rosy,
partly hidden, bluejay-pecked, squirrel-nibbled,
           crawled through by hornets

like the apricot jam on the café table
where I sit now, back in the city. Autumn
haze; cathedral. I witness parents, children
           kiss, tug at parting.

Hard to separate cleanly! Our other apples
cling to the branches. Pick them—you clutch at twigs and
leaves, or just as likely you find that you are
           hoisted and dangling

from the bough. So that by late September,
when the soft fruit long has let go and fallen,
the stern tough tree's loaded with glossy apples,
           hard, dry, and woody

to the tooth; to the eye, globed, rosy beauties.
All the pitiful few we could reach we've picked, but
seen from the roadside the tree is untouched, a virgin
           beaming sheer ripeness.

RIVERSIDE PARK

I've always loved the autumn. Trees bleed amber,
the sun moves south to sink into the river.
For several of these seasons you were here—
if not precisely this noon, bench, or air,
still in New York, October, and inside
my heart. Our timing's trick
was elegantly simple: although sick,
you had not yet died.

How could I resist the chance to share
(shyly at first; more freely the last year)
fusses, ideas, encounters, daily weather?
So for a space we took life in together
reciprocally, since what came your way
you passed along to me.
Experience doubled and then halved kept giving
itself to both as long as both were living.

I pause to watch the afternoon's red ray
advance another notch. Across the way
a mother tends her toddler, and a pair
of strolling lovers vanish in the glare
flung from the river by the westering sun.
I can hardly claim to be alone.
Nevertheless, of all whom autumn's new
russet brocades are draping, none is you.

THE PEACOCK IN THE GARDEN

When the peacock turned
his elegantly coroneted head
to fix me with his gleaming little eye
in order to measure the distance from the patch
of sun-warmed wall, his solitary perch,
to my shoulder where I sat on a low stone bench,

I imagined the thump of a landing, the unwieldy weight,
the pecking beak and massive talons. But
none of this ruffled my tranquility.
Bench and wall and weeping willow tree
wove such a stillness that my reverie
in the peacock's eye achieved assent,
I found in him so much of what I sought.

My silent dead looked out at me from him.
Oceans were coded on his brilliant back;
a deep green forest and a galaxy
were doubly folded in the starry tail
which he would stand and presently unfurl
once he made his mind up to jump down
(not onto me—I'd moved aside a little)
from where he roosted on the sun-warmed wall.

FLESHLY ANSWERS

Doomed beauties, my companions, my familiars,
your long arms braceleted with snakes of danger,

a question twines in all the undergrowth.
How can we tell the living from the dead?

Puvis de Chavannes's tall pearly figures
dressed as sturdy Spartans at the chase

turn out to be pale paper dolls in space.
And how can we be sure that we're alive?

Our bodies, aging, changing, slow and stiffen.
On flesh if not yet quite inert increasingly opaque,

bite or bruise or blemish pose the questions
Where have you been? What have you been doing?

My sister's leg, scaled by a manic cat
nearly three years ago, still is scored and punctured.

Last September I picked blackberries
bare-armed; here are the scratches ten weeks later.

We are passing through the world.
This is some of what it does to us.

A GUST

My bird, oh my beloved,
I live in the fleeting shadow of your wings.
If you have followed me to this quiet place,
you can find me anywhere.
I never need to fear that vacancy.

Late afternoon. Low light whose clarity
spreads you like sunset on the long lagoon,
hovering closer at this amber hour . . .

What do I call a loss as dear as yours,
never to turn at my imploring voice,
luminous, fugitive, embracing silence?
Your presence is a grateful gust of grief,
a wing brush and an echo—oh, an absence.

MAYDAY AT THE FRICK

Sundays the doors don't open until one,
so tourists wait outside in mild spring rain.
The patient, glossily umbrellaed queue
curls round the corner to Fifth Avenue,
confident a few perennials
serenely wait inside: gaunt Cardinals;
a sturdy, swarthy blacksmith bending over
his sooty anvil; a beribboned lover
chasing his lady through espaliered greenery;
a horseman pensive against twilit scenery.
Saint Francis in his stony landscape stands
transfigured, spreading wide his wounded hands.

The human image isn't everywhere.
In a small dim side-room there appear
a jewel-encrusted, flashlight-sized salt cellar,
a massive goblet, and a matching salver;
triptychs, enamels, crucifixes, glass.
Every object closely studied has
not only its own history but a vision,
the artist's rendering of some occasion
that we may never know, but sense, being human,
carrying human baggage. I'm a woman
who just this morning got her period
and now suspects her skirt is stained with blood,
and thus, constrained to keep her raincoat on,
sweats as she moves from room to humid room—
moreover in new shoes, so she can feel
a juicy blister ripening on her heel.
Blood, canvas, blister, silver, sweat, and paint,
a ruined skirt and an ecstatic saint:
none of these incongruities afflicts
my power of seeing. What I see is fixed
all the more firmly, set inside my brain
indelibly, as dried blood leaves a stain.

We have survived the umpteenth winter storm.
It's Mayday, and it's drizzling, but it's warm.
In Central Park the tulips are in bloom.
I also stretch and quicken toward the sun.
For here in the museum I'm not alone
but blessed with a kind companion,
a woman more or less my age, whose eyes
linger on whatever draws my gaze
and vice versa. We seem to pace and pause
and look, speak, laugh obedient to laws—
strong laws, strange ones. A beloved ghost
accompanies us—the brother whom she lost,
who left the world of triptychs, tulips, snow
forever—can it be two years ago?

Her brother and my friend. I see him stand
between us, gesturing with careful hand
at exquisite details we might have missed . . .
he vanishes. It's useless to insist
he stay. We move past Chinese porcelains,
French enamels, statuettes in bronze.
The portraits that look gravely down at us—
were the faces always lined with loss
or do I see them with a different eye?
We've reached the door. It's time to say goodbye.
Once separated, we'll resume our lives
as ordinary women, mothers, wives,
moving through the seasons' gallery
often too rushed to take in what we see.

The rain's evaporated. Hugs; we part.
The man whose face is stamped on either heart,
whose intermittent presence I won't name—
I cannot see him now. But just the same,
he's somewhere near here if he is at all.
Loving what art has made perpetual,
he knew his beauty might be doomed to fade,
but not what skillful human hands had made.

SHELLS

Scalloped synecdoches of satin cloud,
breezes from the Gulf, the creak of wings
(pelicans, egrets, sandpipers), whole coast
portable, rinsable, set out to dry

on towel-draped stools in late afternoon.
Or was the waxing moon already up?
The soft sky throbbed in one long single note
deepening till evening was sore.

Glimmering memento scribbled on a slate
held up between a finger and a thumb,
dry in a twinkling: apricot and pearl
or blurry madras; burgundy and cream,

distaff or wing shape, scoop or lobe or drill.
Listen. A tiny thread of siren song,
note of an unseen bird, or a child's call
to a grandparent (this last the sign

of an affection still reciprocal).
Turning away from the exchange, I drift
over to take a towel, to rinse . . . and then
immediately forget the feeble errand

and find myself drawn back to the warm water.
They cradle me, these fluent twists of color.
A pale pink shell's unspeaking guarantee
cups a kind of convoluted promise

not that the dead will visit—they are dead.
But while we living bathe in such mild air,
neither will I rinse them from my mind,
beloved bones dismantled into sand.

THE BLUE BEAD

In memory of James Merrill

> The world was everything that was the case?
> Open the case.
> —*The Book of Ephraim*

> To keep the blue wave dancing in its prison.
> —"Self-Portrait in a Tyvek Windbreaker"

One of Jimmy's parties. Five at most,
my son is there for once. His gracious host

takes the boy's hand, and leisurely they stroll
over to a table where a bowl

of beach glass gleams in lamplight. "Pick one out,"
the poet says of all these chips of light

subject already to the child's calm gaze.
It doesn't take him long to choose his prize.

"How lovely! Jimmy gave you a blue bead!"
I burble the next morning. Shake of head:

"I chose the bead. He told me I could choose."
All the more, then, a treasure not to lose . . .

. . . but lost by us. That bead is now long gone—
misplaced, no doubt, in the translation

from one place to another, child to boy.
Time's seen to it that my son's memory

of the blue bead by now is buried deep
beneath the fresh experiences that keep

accumulating. I'd forgotten too.
But Jimmy's dying brought it back somehow:

the bowl of glass; the one blue bead bestowed
as choice, not burden; or as something owed

to friendship, and passed on at the behest
of simple kindness to his youngest guest.

I said the gift consisted of that bit
of lambent glass, now lost. But it did not.

Rather, like much that Jimmy left us, this
bead is too clear in memory now to miss,

just as, although the man's returned to air,
his personality is everywhere,

a beacon to me even as I sit
and choose a phrase and cross it out and write

another. Word by word and choice by choice,
this process opens up the jewel case:

the world he left, the words he leaves us too,
so many little globes of radiant blue.

THE RED HAT

It started before Christmas. Now our son
officially walks to school alone.
Semi-alone, it's accurate to say;
I or his father track him on the way.
He walks up on the east side of West End,
we on the west side. Glances can extend
(and do) across the street; not eye contact.
Already ties are feeling and not fact.
Straus Park is where these parallel paths part;
he goes alone from there. The watcher's heart
stretches, elastic in its love and fear,
toward him as we see him disappear,
striding briskly. Where two weeks ago,
holding a hand, he'd dawdle, dreamy, slow,
he now is hustled forward by the pull
of something far more powerful than school.

The mornings we turn back to are no more
than forty minutes longer than before,
but they feel vastly different—flimsy, strange,
wavering in the eddies of this change,
empty, unanchored, perilously light
since the red hat vanished from our sight.

MOM AND DAD

Exactly as I start to feel my son
has outgrown all the things I know but one,
Ethan the neighbors' boy, his summer friend
(he's ten, just for the record; Ethan's nine),
routinely when he speaks to me says Mom.
My husband's Dad. What should new parents do?
Amused but disconcerted, cluck "no, no"?
Matter-of-factly answering to a name
stamps it with confirmation: Here I am.
Feebly we take the path of least resistance
and acquiesce, though not without insistence
that these may not be quite the terms to use
to us. Yet it is churlish to refuse.
Facts of kinship, raw and bald as nature,
rightly yield to friendship's nomenclature.
Our son, his bosom buddy, wields a name,
so Ethan's privileged to do the same.

Still, Mom and Dad don't fail to speculate.
Does Ethan harbor yearnings long unmet?
He has two parents—we're not surrogate.
His Mom and Dad, who live in the next house,
are pleasant, self-contained, seem very . . . nice.
But words betray us, quailing before fact
(neighbor; parent) or compelled to act
as knowledge that can never quite suffice.
Would Ethan's parents speak of us as "nice"?
Well, how would they describe us? Don't ask me.
It's one more boring grown-up mystery.
For children, words mean more than what they say,
for adults less; our interest turns away.
What Ethan claims as bond, possession, dare
dwindles in our indifferent adult air.

What difference should it make to anyone,
to either Mom or Dad, to either son?
Ethan needs to call us something, so
here are two syllables all set to go
and easily pronounced. Forget the whose.
Two apiece allows a child to choose
or keep both—how can one have too much good?
That Dads and Moms *are* good is understood,
taken for granted, by both children still.
(Although this matter's not reciprocal—
a fact both pleasant and mysterious,
our son saves his Mom and Dad for us.)

What is contained in those two syllables?
It's what is in the eye of the beholder,
too precious to disclaim as I grow older;
that single fact my son's not yet outgrown,
and just what Ethan's claiming for his own:
love. Not all; his proper portion,
one strand of childhood summers caught in speech
before the years have swept us out of reach
and, not so long from now, I say to him,
"Remember how you used to call me Mom?"

IDOLATRY BROOD

To gaze at the enormous
yellow moon of summer,
to focus on a stone,
on lives that wax and wane,
on leaves that come undone
in drought or shine with rain,
the child's fresh face, a magnet to the eye—
is this idolatry?

Between the glistening pelts of bathing children
and the knuckle-gnawing refusal
to look up from one's book,
find out some middle way.
Fences. A weathered barn.
Are you getting warmer?
The milky gray expanse of sky implodes
on one more apparition:

no silo shimmering through celestial mist,
only more love for this
world's pillars, banisters,
exit signs, arches, thresholds, winding stairs
struggled up, steep conundrum, toward a truth
hidden even as we breathe the thinner
air and feel the sun's last kiss
blow hot on our closed faces.

THE MYTH OF A HAPPY CHILDHOOD

Out of nowhere these six words have come.
I voice them. I produce them on my tongue.
Then, sitting sweating in the August noon,
I pick up a stone.

Smallish, green, it's one of several
I use to keep the oilcloth, the piled papers
covering the table on the lawn
from flapping in a sudden gust of wind.

To hand and eye the stone is warm and clean.
I hold it to my nose,
then to my mouth. I lick it.
It smells and tastes of city and of rain,

of pavement, first sun-heated and then rinsed.
I put it down,
one side shiny, a more vivid green
where my tongue has been.

If I could somehow know, and know I knew,
how easily (no word fits—
"vision" or "version" or "reality"),
how easily this thing gets jarred, comes loose,

if I could remember how what's crucial
modestly wavers and is pushed aside
in favor of the superficial,
if I could grasp such knowledge in my hand!

But every minute twists
between my fingers, switching shapes with no
more warning than a mood or sky allows
when it turns color. Wind and rain and cloud,

anger, happiness, humidity—
all simply change, without consulting me,
as utterly unable to hold still
as if each were a living thing.

There's no as if. The world
is not inanimate,
so possibilities proliferate.
How should we live our lives from day to day?

What comes forward? What should be held back?
Not that human choice is infinite.
To keep our deep confusions at bay,
most of us concentrate

best on a single emblem at a time.
Whether the brute weight
of human sadness or a broken wing
keeps it pinned down, one monarch butterfly

has fluttered all week feebly on the lawn.
And to embody the enduring myth
of something precious going on and on,
here on the table, solid, warm with sun,

this strangely fragrant stone.

GREEK GOLD

for Joan Mertens

Penises erect if you stoop to squinny,
two rams nose to nose on a golden bracelet
face off. That their bodies have been distilled to
⠀⠀⠀· heads, genitalia

gives the leaps fresh urgency. A demotic
tarnished silver version I bought in Delphi
used to catch my delicate wrist-skin in be-
⠀⠀⠀tween the two muzzles.

Stoically I suffered this painful pinching
for some years; then didn't. My left wrist wore a
watch; the other hand seemed best unencumbered:
⠀⠀⠀I might be writing.

Eros, next, astride a plump dove. Or rather
Erotes, for these are a pair of pendant
earrings. Worn, they both would have swayed, suspended,
⠀⠀⠀the baby rider

leaning forward eagerly, rocking, bobbling,
shadows shifting, cheek onto neck and shoulder
of the wearer at the least hint of motion.
⠀⠀⠀And what is trembling

over here? The earrings sat still; they only
swayed in the soft gusts of imagination.
But this wreath, gold foil, with its oak leaves, acorns,
⠀⠀⠀bee, and cicadas,

faintly shudders even beneath protective
panes of glass: the ahh a bewitched beholder
might expel? A breath from beyond the gallery
⠀⠀⠀stolidly guarded?

No. This subtle quiver inheres in golden
foil and wire we bend to, not in us gazers,
and above all not in what's called the Real World
          beyond the doorway.

Leave the bees half hidden in trembling foliage.
Monumental, in an adjacent corner,
an ornate Italian amphora offers
          white-heightened paintings.

Here's Achilles perched on a little campstool.
Patiently he waits for his new-forged armor
to be handed up to him by the helpful
          sea-nymphs his mother

can command. This nereid holds his helmet;
that one pulls a greave from an unseen warehouse;
still another, parasol-wielding, rides a
          genial dolphin.

Look and look again. Yes, the parasol is
thrust (what insouciance!) through the dolphin's blow hole.
Do real dolphins have blow holes? Is the last nymph
          riding sidesaddle?

I no longer know. But I do remember
overhearing two tour guides. First (to children):
"Is Achilles dressing to go to dinner?
          What are they bringing?"

"Helmet! Shield!" the children reply in chorus.
No one minds, apparently, that he's naked.
Then the second, speculating to adults:
          "Seal-rings so tiny

and details so fine that the master craftsmen
must have employed children." Or were the master
sculptors, carvers, miniaturists, myth-mongers
          all of them children?

If so, taste not just of the time dictated
these winged, bird-footed, lion-pawed Gorgons, Sphinxes,
rampant rams, this chuckling dove-jockey godling,
            but of the makers.

The consumers manifestly were adult.
Were and are. They wore the work of child labor;
gape at these glass cases; buy in the gift shop
            facsimiles—oh,

fairly good, yet lackluster once adorning
creatures such as us: big, unwieldy, mortal,
who eat, sleep, age, worry, and linger over
            representations

of what never was and what is eternal.
Small deft fingers endlessly reinvented
idioms of ornament that translated
            myth into human

artifact and image. The first enchantment
lingers still in copies from my poor bracelet
(now long vanished) to the ones on display here.
            I pass them, leaving

realms of gold, realms mythic and precious, priceless,
for the precincts (how huge and dim they seem now)
of the rest of the Museum first; then stairs; then Fifth
            Avenue. Winter.

STRESS

Philoctetes' venom-sodden foot;
Job's boils no potsherd scraping can relieve;
Amfortas' wound, forever festering—
men suffer for no reason plain to see.
Now, stoic in the scarlet leotard
of eczema, you join their company.

Like Philoctetes' shipmates, like the friends
taking Job to task for what foul crime,
confronted with affliction we think blame
and promptly diagnose it with a name.
Angry eruptions, back and flanks—oh yes,
no one hesitates to name the cause.

The etiology is love gone wrong,
turned inside out. To love, be loved in turn,
never a simple matter, has become
the seamy side, all bristle, itch, and sting,
desire's dynamic somehow gone amok
halfway between skeleton and skin.

Rage, frustration, disappointment, loss—
what's not concealed beneath that flagrant cloak?
Or rather less a mantle than a germ
which once it penetrates the outer layer
won't settle for oblivion again
but hovers hungry somewhere in the air.

Anywhere. In the Butler Library mural
Athena shines, wrapped in her 3-D aegis.
Bald green demons on each side of her
lower and clutch. I would have named them Fear,
Ignorance, Prejudice—but now all these
seem secondary to this new disease

whose absence must be our idea of health,
celestial serenity, a cool
and unmarked carapace, exterior
radiant with complacency, proclaiming
a mind of luminous tranquility,
a body open to the world's regard.

THE OYSTER GRAIN

Think of the ancient fable. Wound and bow
    conspired to cause a flow
of honeyed art to minister to pain—
    skill caused by nothing else than suffering
it also helped to heal. There may be no
    heroes today, but there remain
similar cycles: sting transformed to song.

The song stands firm. Shrunken, perhaps, is scale,
    not mode or key but whole
occasion for the singing to begin.
    The sudden flash, the wounded self-esteem
still make exquisite music, but how small
    and narcissistic, fragile, thin
it all becomes if self is the sole theme!

Made miniature, the metamorphosis
    must work its art from this
pale oyster bed, a single human soul.
    Yet once the incantation has begun
weaving its spell, see! magic still can bless
    both particular and whole
worlds of feeling. All turns into pearl.

Bedded in fleshy tissue, fold on fold,
    whose puckered layers hold
the guilty grain and the surrounding wound,
    each oyster shell exists to mask its grit.
The stubborn jaws clamp tight as if to scold
    any intruder who might sound
the soft interior, dare to handle it—

double defense of what is cupped within,
    since a tough filmy skin
already shrouds the central spore of sand
    from such assaults as ocean's slop and drench
or any wetness vaguely leaking in
    or—worse—an actual human hand
outstretched to coax, seduce, caress, or wrench

the clasped lips open. No: this incubation
    permits no violation.
The ripening young pearl is darkly nursed
    through hidden conduits that filter dangers.
Locked lids conceal incessant transformations:
    the seed immersed, again immersed,
rinsed and re-bathed in crystallizing angers.

No Trespassing into the shady cave—
    rule causing me to have
continual dreams of things turned inside out.
    At some dark door a figure stands, observes
as one by one old carrots, blankets, loves
    are brusquely held up to a light
that shines through every weary knot of nerves.

All kinds of rummaging! The hag who stole
    our bed—sheets, pillows, all—
from Broadway and a Hundred and Sixteenth Street;
    me washing dirty linen on my knees;
the two of us unloading drawers of stale
    refrigerator-haggard fruit—
what but illicit entrances are these?

Or take the summer cottage. Its warped door,
    a perfect target for
cold hungry hunters trekking through the snow,
    is raped one winter night by god knows who.
Anonymous tracks still stride across the floor.
    Oh, all's now fixed: I live with you
in the same house. Some things we'll never know.

Slowly spring mud-time slogged the footprints under.
　　Distance dulled the anger.
Next time we'll not allow a single glass
　　pane in the door—the window? Some opaque
substitute substance, gloomier but secure,
　　might make a fortress of a house
but couldn't be seen through and wouldn't break.

Or else an eerie mirror glazes all
　　the world into one small
figure receding down the corridors
　　of ghostly mansions. Skeleton or key?
It squinnies into scores of cellar holes
　　(closets, memories, doors),
crowing triumphantly "All eyes are me!"

Shut the grim vista. Let the jewel roll free
　　of its rank reverie
only when dreams have wrung their dramas dry
　　as laundry sweetening in air and sun.
When metaphoric ingenuity
　　can innocently meet an eye,
let floodgates open and the gem wash down

the purling stream sprung from that bed of pain.
　　Of course there will remain
the oyster shell, potential residence
　　for the next tenant. Any wounding day
can deeply seed a tiny pearl again—-
　　destined, like mythic rose or toad, to fall
once ripened from our mouths and roll itself away.

ON MYTH

Its view is simultaneous
discovery and reminiscence.
—Mona Van Duyn

I

For myth's enduring freshness,
its dewy youth, five reasons come to mind.
First, myth concerns itself with origins.
"The recent flood had softened earth to ooze,"
writes Victor Hugo of the time of Ruth,
and people shrank in fear from "giant foot prints."
That balmy night, while Ruth and Boaz snoozed,
a brontosaurus lumbered through the mire.
Dinosaur Bible? Virgin territory.
Thus poets breathe new life into a story.
Two: in myth the idea of storytelling
itself is new. The listeners, young and old,
thirst to hear, believe what they are told.
Three: the protagonists of mythic tales—
gods, goddesses, nymphs, heroes—
are mostly young and beautiful forever.
Granted, some few are ugly, weak, or old,
and some are young and beautiful and die;
such exceptions merely prove the rule.
Four: the timeless or historical
present is the medium of myth,
matrix of verities new, old, unchanging.
Everything that happens thus is happening
both over and over and for the first time.
Five: we have all been thrust into some scene—
seminar, office, wedding, waiting room—

possessed of much less background than we need
to navigate (one or two introductions,
a smattering of genealogy,
cosmology, geography) and still
make do. Just so, we enter into myth
unequipped, all but naked, yet familiar.
No family tree of the Olympians
greets us; we have to work it out ourselves
by means of clues, allusions, disguises.
Being unprepared, we have to wing it.
And from the anxious flapping of our wings
a great gust rises, pages start to turn,
reanimated stories stir again—
changeable, fickle, never written down
like history in one capacious tome;
rather what poets try to stay alert for,
in search of which they travel a long way,
catch part of in midair, in part make up,
at once create, remember, steal, and know.

II

Myth used to seem to me like stone
or truth—that tough, countable on
to stand there absolutely still
while we could move around at will,
wandering vaguely through the maze
of summer's green meandering days,
now poking at the compost heap,
now in the hammock fast asleep
and in each long luxurious dream
entering myth's sublime domain.

Myth isn't flesh; but it's not stone.
It has a nature all its own.
Our human version of reality
insists on restlessness, vitality,
requires that we laugh, cry, speak,
grieve and desire, sleep and wake,
answer to cries of father, mother,
scurry from one place to another-
as if significance were proved
by the mere fact of having moved.

Myth has no need of motion, though,
to enter into all we do.
Startling in its intimacy,
personal as apostrophe,
bristling with proper names,
rival traditions, counter-claims,
conservative yet transitory,
with room for every human story,
myth is the rumor we pass on
after due revision.

Feeding on incident, myth waits
while life on life accumulates;
or it may on the contrary
flash forth its mythhood suddenly.
Epiphanies sound good in rhyme
but myth cannot be boxed in time.
It's outside time—custodian of
the huge kaleidoscope of love
and death that turns a bit each minute
so subtly we forget we're in it.

ON THAT MOUNTAIN

Evidence everywhere: accumulation.
Leaves atremble and narratives of branches
ramifying, so ever more connections
stay unfinished nor ever to be finished.
Do we not all have separate destinations?
Not that it matters. Aching opalescence
held us all spellbound, motionless, atingle,
balanced like sun and rain before a rainbow,
thunder purring and lightning white as daylight.
After the storm passed, all the world was gleaming,
glossy, almost lubricious with potential,
each blade of grass a dagger in the morning,
each leaf a goblet, brimming, winking, ready
to repay some small measure of night's thunder.
Couples stood tiptoe, trembling at departure,
kissing, breathing *Oh, let me touch your wisdom;*
let me then taste reciprocally your beauty.
More than mere iridescence—transformation.
Recall the dark face, thunder cowled at midnight.
Recall the bright face, rinsed clean for separation
as we're making our several preparations,
so many roads diverging in the greenwood,
putting on the inevitable blinders—
I must keep to my path and my path only—
closing our ears to thunder and cicadas,
closing our eyes to all those trembling branches,
meekly turning our backs on opalescence,
on the jewels of potential transformation,
getting ready to go back down the mountain.

THE HERMIT

And may at last my weary age
Find out the peaceful hermitage . . .
Till old experience do attain
To something like prophetic strain.
        —Milton, "Il Penseroso"

April, May, and finally June.
We'll meet again, but not too soon!
Show you my poem . . . keep in touch . . .
call me tomorrow . . . It's too much.
Too wide a web becomes a curse.
(Spider or victim, which is worse?)
A word-web, true; no heavier stuff.
Language, though, is strong enough.
Yet language rather than event
being my homeland, I consent
each autumn to re-poise my pen,
plunge in the maelstrom once again.

But summer! Time to turn that leaf
over and take a good long breath.
Reticence is the season's code.
It's time to wander down the road
unnoticed; time to disappear
stealthily as a used-up year.
It's time to feel the heaviness
of passing hours that curse and bless
like boredom on an endless day:
clouds chase the sun across the sky,
but when the light begins to die
you feel a shadow of regret
which you immediately forget.
Day slid across the Sunday lawn
so slowly; now that day is gone.

Writing things down, I used to feel,
saved them, and also made them real.
Dull cucumbers submerged in brine
turn to tart pickles, given time.
Writing and friendship? All the better
motive for a friendly letter!
To write a letter; to extract
some essence from the daily act
of repetition, one must pry
the cover off, and boldly try
to plumb the depths of thought and word.
One doesn't have to be a bard
to scoop a cupful from the hoard.
A harmless impulse, then. Why not,
if in the mood, sit down to write?
Yet it's become apparent how
this act is not so harmless now.
Even to jot a casual line
seems somehow like a waste of time
when Reader A commands the sum
of all I think and feel and am
and B knows nothing. Either way,
must I evoke painstakingly
the sky as shiny as a plate,
the chugging of a lobster boat
now disappearing round the cove,
the hooing of a mourning dove?
Must I spell out in slow detail
each sound, each smell, each sharp-edged sail?

One purpose of cohabitation,
I've finally learned, is relaxation
from the imperative to describe
each seashell bared by each low tide.
(Describe to whom? I never said
for years, just blithely went ahead.)
In our domain of restfulness
there's often nothing to express.
Myriad foam-tongues lick the rock
we sit on, silent, back to back.

Our mutual abstractedness
is like a conjugal caress,
familiar, absent-minded, fond,
both confident and oddly blind.
What's in your mind I understand
surely as if you'd squeezed my hand
or winked at me; but much of you
is often wholly out of view.
Yet how can conversation cope
with consciousness' relentless tape?
How can mere chitchat freeze the flux?
A brook that burbles over rocks
is easier to catch and tame,
certain each handful is the same,
than the unfurling colored strip
of passing instants. Try it. Dip
the language ladle gently down
and spoon up contemplation,
alphabet soup that overflows
with all the moment sees and knows,
a potable kaleidoscope
of past and future, fear and hope.
Spoon after spoonful pours the source
of imperfection's tragic force.
And yet my preference is for
an utterance that aims at more—
a single splendid edifice,
not an untidy humble nest,
though both are made of the same stuff,
our ever-raveling human cloth.
We snatch—to speak, to write, to hear—
meanings that never quite come clear.
George Herbert says "Thy Word is all,"
though he does add "if we could spell."
But all the symbols we can read
are hairs on one great bushy head,
are tiny ripples in a pool
tumultuously illegible.
In order to begin to spell
one must sit absolutely still.

And thus the hermit in her cell
(although this hermit may be me
or anyone, let's call her She)
requires hermetic solitude
so she can parse the golden wood,
the dying leaves that drift and fall
obedient to autumn's rule,
the stars, that twinkling alphabet
decipherable only late.
Her study is the endless text
collating this world and the next,
till letter-perfect at the last
in this celestial spelling test,
she sounds it out: i n f i n i t y
emblazoned on the starry sky.
Infinity—yet limited
by what can fit into one head,
old papers folded up unread,
whether because they're too well known
to need perusing once again
or that they ask more world and time
than even a hermit wants to spare,
that reticent philosopher
whose gaze at daybreak takes each blade
and stalk and petal god has made,
whom nightfall finds with wrinkled brow
scanning Orion and the Plough.
Infinite Heaven is immense.
But only earth bestows the sense
of something out of human reach
rippling into endless speech.
What she's forgotten she has known,
so somehow thus it's still her own,
whereas the old prophetic strain
warns her that mysteries remain
and that in life's sheer dailiness
that strain turns swiftly into stress.

To prophesy is not to see
a map of future clarity;
rather it means a vision
of things both done and to be done.
At length we learn what we believe,
probably just in time to leave
the endless party. At the door
who wouldn't pause to ask for more?

How to deny our hungry need
for company as much as bread?
Weary our age may be, but how
many will venture what Thoreau
lived and what Milton recommends?
Are we prepared to forgo friends?
The former was a misanthrope;
the latter's is a cautious hope
or aspiration, like a prayer,
few other people seem to share.

Other people. What of them,
that net of squabbles, family, home?
Affections and traditions too
are caught there. But can one see through
the snarls and knots of tangled lives,
the needs of children, husbands, wives
to the serenity of bare
celestial statements in midair?
The hermit thinks: if I discard
companionship it will be hard.
But only in this silence can
I gather up the strength to scan
the mesh of meanings overhead
and underfoot, recall the dead
and love the living for a while
until again I start to spell
a longer word than I can quite
decipher, and could never write.
Let my mind be a simple brush
rapidly sketching, in the hush

of trees and bird song, fugitive
sketches of how it felt to live,
a "dear companion" (Valéry)
"of silence" living next to me.
Milton perhaps would not approve,
but even hermits fall in love.
Or lovers, living parallel,
can both sit down and try to spell
till old experience makes a true
hermit of either me or you.

THE POLES

Present and past: opposing entities
alike in sharing evanescences.
Neither can we grasp and hold with ease.
Despite occasional blips of clarity,
both continually slip away.

I want my mother. Where is she?
She is the garden, I could grandly say.
Underfoot. Or growing in that tree.
Ubiquitous, and nowhere to be found.
You might as well try to lasso the wind.

You might as well attempt to catch the air
and bottle, label, lock it up somewhere.
What's gone refuses to recur.
Carpe diem (pluck the day
as if it were a flower; pay

attention only to what's palpable)?
No sooner do we try to drink our fill
at this minute's fountain than we reel
and drift away from here to there, the vast,
vague, forgiving vista of the past.

Back and forth we teeter in between
two poles, two worlds, the seen and the unseen,
antagonists, what is vs. what has been,
bracketers of the place
that we inhabit, if time equals space.

ALONG EDGES

to Mark Rudman

> The poet is the true and only doctor.
> —Emerson

Scientist of mourning, doctor, teach
me your categories. Which is which—
the tragic and the comic and bizarre
melting to one, the fishing boat, the bar,
the fearful father shining like a star?
You see beyond the visual, you know.
Each meaning yields its antitype to you:
life out of death and nothing out of all.
Blackness that opened with your father's fall
spreads into a dark screen against which glow
those paltry episodes we glibly call
the present. In your presence, hovering things
materialize—but not to fold their wings,
perch on a shoulder. No, they prophesy
scenes off limits to the daily eye.
Funny or uncanny, wild or tame,
your rapt abstraction holds you just the same.
Give you a death and even as you grieve,
you pull life like a bright scarf from your sleeve,
wave it once vaguely in the cloudy air—
soon memories are showing everywhere.
The ordinary opens its dull door,
no violence is alien any more,
your golden son is dancing on a tomb
you traveled far to see but fear to climb.
You see yourself at twenty; equally
see all our absences a century
from now, when not a single soul of all
our cohorts will be here. For good or ill,
now is our time, this strange earth is our place.
Each present moment like a glint of ice

above opacities of ocean shows
deeper intimations from below.
With so much dimly grasped at, how can all
be somehow seen and understood? You feel
the double pull of gravity and joy
and felt it years ago, a lawless boy
out in pursuit of knowledge, drink, or sin,
wandering along edges looking in.

Poet of mounds and ruins, prairies, caves,
of deserts glittering in the sun's raw waves,
of childhood asthma and of city snow,
Riverside Park and Courbet's studio,
the unmade movie always being shot
at the sheer cliff's side, whether "real" or not,
I send you greetings from my patch of green,
magician of the seen and the unseen,
to whom the truth of memory adheres
through country stillnesses and city fears.
Seeing your lit window, I can tell
the war against oblivion's going well.
The spotlight of your desk lamp is a clue
to secrets I will learn of first from you.

SEARCHING THE SCRIPTURES

Sunny May morning; going through the mail.
Among solicitations, one stands out
from summer neighbors: a Conquer-a-thon—
so many laps jogged; dollars pledged per lap.
The logo on the Union Christian Baptist
·School's envelope: a bearded helmeted
head; a scroll reading CONQUERORS; below it
in smaller letters Rom. 8:37.

Last week I finally did it: gave away
the hefty dictionary a dear friend
had, among many other volumes, left me.
Let the book table at the school's spring fair
dispose of it! I had no space to spare.
His Bible, though, comparatively svelte,
I'd kept—no doubt for such contingencies.
To check the reference is a moment's work,
except I pause a little at the fly leaf:
First Unitarian Church of Cleveland.
September 15, 1968.
Above these lines, Presented to: a blank
filled by his name.
Here is the Epistle. *Nay*, writes Paul,
in all these things we are more than conquerors
through him that loved us.

I sit, the Bible open on my lap.
Then, as I move to shut the book again,
a small pink slip of paper flutters out—
an office memo, blank. But on the back
a few words printed in a familiar hand:
Luke 12:49–53.
Clearly it is premature to close
this mystic tome without a second time
checking a reference. I flip to Luke,
not without some sense of what I'll find.

Sure enough, this passage is in red.
Divinity is talking; listen up!
Vermilion words float off the page like smoke:
I am come to send fire on earth.
And what will I, if it be already kindled?
Then, testily: *Suppose ye I am come*
to give peace on earth? I tell you Nay,
but rather division. The father
shall be divided against the son
and the son against the father.

As is well known, the book is so constructed
scenarios concocted come undone,
reshuffle, recombine, float free again
to constellate in yet another shape.
Fragments of plot, divided families
sparkle on the surface of a sea
boiling bloody myriads have drowned in.
Or does that sea politely part to let
a virtuous remnant pass? This piece of paper
ripped from the story, torn from medias res,
a family drama or a cooling rage,
is what I hold of my dead friend this minute.
I turn the blushing faces of the code
back toward each other, shut the book
and shelve it with its secret still intact.
Its many secrets.

Union Christian Baptist
Conquer-a-thon. $1.50 might
possibly be sufficient per lap.
Ethan, who will be running, just turned ten.

PERFORMANCES, ASSORTMENTS

Quotes are from Hart Crane's poems
"Possessions," "Recitative," and "The Tunnel"

"Performances, assortments, resumés":
I see these rubrics or their variations
plastered on lampposts in the neighborhood
daily. Sixty years ago, you died.
Were you predicting, or did you just see,
vatic, distracted, how the city spoke
in disembodied voices, Faxes, numbers?
Performances, assortments: these deploy
a whole cast of accomplishments and lies,
keys and keyholes, questions, claims, and answers
gathered, dispersed, exhibited for what
future consumption every passerby
has the potential hunger to determine.
Itch and impulse dictate what to choose.
City as marketplace . . . Did resumé
already in the twenties mean curriculum
vitae, as it does now? I assume so;
and assortment brings to mind hors d'oeuvres,
life's feast as restaurant offering. Aha!
Presentation: that's the word I want,
fumbling for denominators. Market,
exchange, bazaar, everything on display,
strutted, touted, but at a remove.
Whatever, Hart, was there was there for sale,
flapping like a flag from Baudelaire
listlessly on its mooring of Scotch tape.

You saw beyond advertisements. Behind
each paper face lurked splittings of the soul,
its mask or its persona. "Janus-faced
capture," or—grotesque arresting image
suggesting mutilation and impalement
but also somehow exhibition,

a spit revolving in a restaurant window
closely watched by hungry passersby—
"I, turning, turning on smoked forking spires."
So much for writhing; but you then went on
"The city's stubborn lives, desires." Precisely:
that flaky wealth of choices and assortments
daily presented like a bill of fare.

In the face of all these riches, how
to stay, to be one person in one skin?
The city's whole dynamic says Divide,
proliferate, diversify. And then?
"Twin shadowed halves: the breaking second holds
In each the skin alone, and so it is
I crust a plate of vibrant mercury
Borne cleft to you, and brother in the half."
Performances, assortments. In the press
and anonymity of quick desire
shuttling between worlds, did you feel
Wordsworth of all people touched the truth
when he wrote "a tree of many one"?
Not tree, not in New York, but anything
of many one, and one becoming many.
Assortments, resumés: our several selves
floating like ticker tape to what parade
of the unnamable? Each marcher turns
and asks to see the goods. Performances?
The face, the Janus faces, are your own.

AT THE TEMPEST

In the long speech that bores Miranda so
(she's not alone; our son is yawning too),
Prospero tells how his younger brother
learned to take charge; first one task, then another,
granting this suit, rejecting that, and so
finally unseating Prospero.
No sooner has Miranda fallen asleep,
numbed with minutiae of statesmanship,
than, spark-like, an idea seems to leap
from your head into mine. I all but know
the parallel that has occurred to you:
a certain bustling colleague's machinations,
memos, behind-the-scenes manipulations
not in Milan but here. We'll be comparing
notes later; but the pleasures of this sharing,
acrid, intangible, delicious, all
persist after the first loud curtain call—

when something hollow in the long applause
reminds me of the ghosts in Shakespeare's house.
Two theater lovers in particular,
though both are dead, contrive to be right here:
Tony, whose tiny place on Thompson Street
was papered with old Playbills; bittersweet
beautiful Charlie, he whose watchful wit
observed a scene while still arranging it,
foreshadowing Patrick Stewart's Prospero—
somber magician making the play go.

English teachers, back when I was young,
proclaimed a purity that now feels all wrong.
The jagged plot line (climax; denouement)
loomed then like an iceberg, tall and gaunt.
If such a world, schematic, classic, clear,
existed once, it doesn't any more;
advancing years chase clarity away,

or objectivity has had its day.
Sit in a theater as the lights go down:
what sets the scene is garnered from one's own
experience, whose resonance is blurred,
so many echoes bounce off every word.
A stray line may evoke a memory
of conversation earlier that day.
The abstract Theme I once was taught to seek
lodges in some incident last week,
reemerging as the actors speak.
Thus saturated with the personal,
art can provide the old vicarious thrill
through recognition and acknowledgement,
the sense that we are part of what is meant—
as when, forgetting one another's name,
two people nod in passing just the same:
an inward smile, a private gleam, and on
into the evening where a crescent moon,
old and new, familiar and strange,
tilts in the twilight, sentinel of change.

Art's entertainment? Art is a device,
a valve for siphoning the extraneous,
channeling the foamy overflow
of what my high school English teachers knew
as Truth, a concept out of fashion now.
They mapped it, graphed it, plotted it for me,
but I can't pass it on so tidily.
For the epiphanies that art affords
may come disguised, without the help of words,
masked in likeness, fanged and clawed with pain,
or giggling, gulping, flowing like spring rain.

WINGED WORDS

Trying to speak means flailing with
gestures half-sculpted out of need,
eloquent in the way of myth—
monumental, hard to read.
How does anything get said?
A nascent, feebly struggling thought,
hard to collect and to recover,
contrives to spit its substance out.
Words are the wings that lift us over.

Garbling a recollected tongue,
swamped in simultaneity,
latecome words go down among
syllables learned by the age of three.
Look light kitty love you me—
for every flight from the teeth's gate,
as Homer has it, others are
prisoners, crying "Let us out,
out of this dumbness, away from here!"

See me, poised and ready for
writing the words that cluster round.
My moving pen is an open door
releasing syllable into sound.
Sprung from dumbness by my hand,
a few words fly. By some stern law
of choice or chance the empty air
fills—with what I scarcely know.
Writing it down might make it clear.

Words are flighty. But once set down,
utterances give form to life,
celebrate pleasure, focus pain.
Every writer wields a knife
sharp with danger. Nothing's safe.
When offered up to clarity,
memory acquires mysterious power.
With each i dotted and each crossed t,
intimate histories appear.

Is it for love of you I read
your sentences as points of pain,
or does attention always breed
phantoms of meaning like a stain?
Show me that page you wrote again.
Now I sense an undertow
drawing you far away from here.
What you felt and saw and knew
crosses the paper like a scar.

A child is curled in his mother's arm.
The lamplit page or hammock's sway
create a zone exempt from harm,
devoted to one kind of play.
Dream all night and read all day.
Tell it again, the precious tale
of what we lose, seek, reacquire.
Sunset again. The sky goes pale.
A great page flickers with words of fire.

Eye usurps mind and mouth. Exclusion
of idle chat holds death at bay.
Silence allows no clear conclusion
except she has no more to say.
Today's no different from yesterday.
Read her the news; or improvise,
when you can bear to read no more,
some speech that needs no lips or eyes.
Conversation is metaphor.

The lips are locked. What else is left?
I can no longer read the gaze.
Pity for a life bereft
of power to tell, amuse, amaze . . .
Reduced to stillness, year-long days
pass in a fog of who can tell?
I'd say the password's Nevermore.
Other conclusions loom as well.
What was language ever for?

All we have done, all we will do—
helplessly we write and read,
opening the veins of what we know.
Even when pain is understood
the mildest scribble may draw blood.
Why does the dark authority
of written language reassure?
This fearful self is more than me.
Our words are bodies. We write on air.

Words are the wings that lift us over
out of this limbo, away from here.
Writing it down might make it clear.
Intimate histories appear,
cross the paper like a scar.
A great page flickers with words of fire.
Conversation is metaphor.
What was language ever for?
Our words are bodies. We write on air.

HALFWAY DOWN THE HALL

Bruno Bettelheim observes somewhere
that autistic children in his care
reduce domestic articles to their

lowest denominator. Thus (he wrote)
butter became *grease,* sugar *sand.* I quote
this sketchily remembered anecdote

from one of the Anchor Books that would arrive
in our apartment on Riverside Drive
back when both my parents were alive.

My sister was in college; I was still
in school. Hard-backed books adorned the tall
dining room shelves; paperbacks filled a hall

so dark that Dickens, whom I read that year,
evoked a world not too dissimilar
to the general gloom of our ground floor

quarters. Reinvented in my head,
Bleak House and *Little Dorrit* as I read
rearranged themselves on Morningside

Heights. In our dim hallway many more
dusty discoveries were still in store:
Bentley and Brecht, Ionesco, Yourcenar,

Jann Kott, Jung, Lucian, Esslin, Harold Bloom,
Woolf and Forster (each in their own room),
Arendt and Freud and Bruno Bettelheim.

So was I happy, crouching in the nook
halfway down the hall, nose in a book,
from half a lifetime later, looking back?

Wrong word. I was alive, at work, at play.
But why the long digression, you may say?
And why exhume this semi-memory?

Because Alzheimer's—yes, senility—
or midlife intimations anyway
make it hard to process what I see.

Grown strange through too much familiarity,
everything specific falls away.
I have to grope for what I want to say;

it still emerges alien. The other day,
riding home tired on the IRT,
I looked up from my book. Across from me

a woman read a Bible bound in black
with gilt-edged pages. *Oh, a silver book*
was how I took this in. Then my next look:

Woman in woven poncho. Hot; perspires.
My only thought is *little woolen squares*
as if geometry is what she wears.

All this may be a tempest in a tea—
pot. We may be barking up the wrong tree,
Bettelheim and I. How easily

he could have jotted down illegibly
"autistic" for "artistic"—as could I.
(One least misreading, and how rapidly

the changes spread! "To dream; aw, there's the rub,"
a student paper says that Hamlet said.)
Bettelheim cannot help me; he is dead.

Biographers now start to claim, indeed,
in life he bullied, beat his patients, lied
about his past. Debate flares: was he good

or bad? His tale may all be an invention.
I don't care. My disbelief's suspension
reveals a stubborn little core of fiction

(autistic or artistic, either way,
the children at that table cleverly
recast the shape of what they had to say)

or fable, tough as truth. We do erase
the quiddity of substance, sacrifice
precision. Names, like labels, do come loose,

fall off, and get replaced. And day by day
the normal nourishment of brain and eye
flickers toward invisibility.

AUGURIES

Impatient with what's visible,
human illusion turns to trope.
The crucial news is illegible,
spelled out in letters of alien shape.
The mind becomes a catacomb
sheltering snatches of repose.
Successive icons of lost time
totter like rows of dominoes.

Talkers are lowering their voices,
but dialectic drums its fingers
restlessly. The attention pauses,
notes how a graceful image lingers.
From dancing school to funeral,
silken banners gaily flutter.
Occasions that appear quite real
turn out to be phantasms later.

Maps at midnight, outposts gleam
for travelers in search of light,
who stumble, stub their toes on gloom,
wander lost into the night.
They wake up aching in empty rooms.
Where is memory's white arch?
What mocking spirits fueled their dreams,
only to scuttle out of reach?

Affections wither and fall away.
Bone dry, polished as a vase,
I watch the January sky.
Sunlight enters the room like grace.
Sill and armchair, bookcase, door
are sliced by the blade of winter sun.
Silently across the floor
stalk the fingers of afternoon.

FALCON

Stumbling along a sidewalk clogged with snow,
I don't see him, then suddenly I do.
He pops from nowhere in the blizzard's wake,
gesticulates, guffaws, then turns to walk
the way I'm going, "so that we can talk."
He does all the talking—wants to tell
me of an apparition on his sill
that morning. "Talons! Wingspan of four feet!"
It seems some hefty bird of prey alit
and beat its wings across the windowpane—
not albatross, not eagle, but their kin.
I'm asking some vague question or other;
he interrupts. "The falcon was my mother.
Funny, huh." It's not a question; he
demands acknowledgement. And I agree;
I think the falcon was his mother too.
That's settled; his decoding must be true.
We smile, then turn and trudge our separate ways,
negotiating strata of mixed grays.

Metaphor and myth and déjà vu;
romantic notions of madness, too.
Wingstroke: the cruel diagonal, the slash
of entry into time, the gory gash
inflicted by a visionary claw
on winter's blankness. What was it he saw?
Wings agitated in their little storm,
a private blizzard in the public one,
swoosh of arrival or epiphany?
I don't dispute that some reality

alighted on his window sill. I see
his face light up: relief at recognition.
The vision came; he recognized the vision.
His wounds may still be throbbing. All the same,
he's like a person who retrieves a name
or crucial clue that he had thought was gone
from the fierce blizzard of oblivion.

TWELFTH BIRTHDAY

As if because you lay
(*deeply embarrassing*) inside
my body, I could (*inconceivable*)
follow your swift thoughts into their blue
immersion even now,
stilettoes flickering, or schools of fish
maneuvering, first clear and then occluded,
though now and then a piercing gleam cuts through;

as if the snow reflections that glaze
the winter afternoon to porcelain
could penetrate the secrets of a skull
that happens to have lodged (*improbable*)
inside me once. Your liberation
twelve years ago today is the occasion
you and your friends are celebrating now
behind a door that's firmly shut.

The fantasy you've lately been devouring
features an evil mage with hourglass eyes.
Last week, when you were furious at me
(I must have thrown some precious thing away),
you swiftly slipped into your parents' room
and turned the bedside clock an hour ahead.
Discovered as the culprit, wickedly
you smiled. You knew time was my enemy.

MUTABILITY

What is it that always rearranges
the scenery? Not lack of appetite.
We love the world as it is, and then it changes.

Like a massive door on silent hinges
swinging open to reveal some sight
our next blink abruptly rearranges,

each fresh glimpse first shows and then estranges.
Reality is this and then is that.
Stay just the way you are, world! But it changes.

Everything unknown at first entrances,
shimmering with dangers, clues, and doubt
experience organizes, rearranges.

Drab is familiar. Glamorous is strange.
We drink them in as time is running out,
loving the world as it is until they change,

laws of space or logic of romances.
Life lies ahead of us and then does not.
Something inexorable rearranges
the scene we thought we knew, and the world changes.

from **Starting from Troy** (1975)

THE FALL OF TROY

Sing now the heavy furniture of the fall,
the journey's ending. Strong Aeneas bears
deep on his shoulders all the dark wood chairs
and tables of destruction. Bruising, blunt,
they force his feet on up the war-scraped hills
past raped dead temples. All Achilles kills
litters the trail of sofa legs with other
endings of houses. Further up, gods sit
changing their own upholsteries of deceit,
ordaining shelves and benches as the goal
of his dim voyage. Sometimes arrows drawn
on chair backs point the way they must go on,
signs that some corridor of destiny
is reserving him a threshold. Aeneas weeps
at wind or passion, but steadfastly keeps
carrying battered merchandise marked ROME
in one direction, pondering it all.

SAPPHO, KEATS

The girls in Lesbos have dark eyes
and scorn to play their natural role.
Flowers don't photosynthesize
on beach and field there, blooming damp
and rich in moonlight. Mushroom-pale
they must have been, but Sappho saw
what flowers blossomed at her feet.
Another nighttime poet sniffed
instead of looking: cold-stunned eyes
failed in his fragrant darkness, where
he flew (those viewless wings!) through sweet
remindful beacons of the air.
I think the impulses were one,
some rooting down of love, like wheat,
in the unjilting bed of ground.

SUPER NIVEM

Asperges me hyssopo, et super nivem dealbabor.
—Psalm LI

My scars are slow in healing, dark
thin crowns of wound where none should be,
marring what wraps me, marring me.

I am not sad at anything,
not stung, but scars remember more
and make me veteran of a war

I fought forgetting. Stenciled on
wide unresisting planes of skin,
they trace my alphabet of sin,

the language undeciphered still.
But clotted letters I can read.
They mark the parts of me that bleed.

DADDY

These weeks, and up and down, and it goes on.

Stay off it for six weeks, one said.
No. Only pulling at the past
can bring me up to what is dead.
Let me write elegies at least,
I said, and then wrote nothing down.

But no forgetting. Elegies
were all around me: youth and age together
or some botched love or any reaching out
meant you and me and death. No need to write.

Breaking the silences and spaces took
more than the violence of time. A fierce
loneliness pushed us in and out of town.
Country and city: what we fled would follow.

Dead people, no, they don't come back.
That's why they're dead, one said.

It pulled together slowly. What must be
still disentangled was the reason first
for seeing things at all
                                        so far away
and never farther than my arms and legs
and never coming back. No, no forgetting.
It would be funny, if I loved you less,
life's lavish spread of food for elegies.

THAT TIME, THIS PLACE

All terribly remembered towers of Troy,
this too known house cries out for you.

Priam gone the rest of the sons and daughters
bickering in porticoes reciting
anecdotes by now catalogues of failed
glories slaughters or triumphs lost downtown
half tragedies of cousins scrutinized

fossils of families and fates of war:
the shell remains, the softer parts decay

How did he say goodbye? What rests with us?
the sad unbaked enamel of the past

no low-relief medallions of farewells
tableaux left unassembled   no forebodings
for framing pictures   did he hope for this?
Undemolished palace, children few, but those
knowing every weary pore of the others.
How well we see our failures!
we know each other's sadness ever better
companionship is what we have and we hate it
we mural of survivors

                              tableaux left unassembled
there on the tower sun in his eyes he said
or in the hall at twilight with wine
something about winning losing going
nothing came after

softer parts decay,
the shell remains, and I know every angle
of wall to floor, the smell of all the mornings,
seasons, meals, radiators   Coalesce,
poor jigsaw past, or come apart, poor present.
What hero won what battle once upon
and so forth   crickets creaking in the twilight
of unremembered days

What rests with us?
How did he say goodbye? Did he say it?
Or must we build what was by tearing down
what is, beat down our celebrated towers
to our own stature, shut our eyes, and sing?

All fighters, fathers, all departed heroes,
our house cries out for you.

from **Slow Transparency** (1983)

ALIEN CORN

Turn to a blustery March where Cinderella
sits on a metal bedstead near a beach
sifting and sorting lentils. Ostrogoths
swagger the shingled village's one street.
Roaring of south wind. Vomited-up wine
splotches the floor near her corner.
Tiny red glass beads and shards of something
among the lentils slow her fingers further.
As in a fairy tale, the careful task,
to put together, to extract, complete
a testing chore by whom or why imposed
is unrecorded, as is the reward.
The needle may be pulled gleaming from the haystack,
the last lentil clatter clean into the pan—
she lacks the unimagined talisman
needed to pace and trace the labyrinth
bobbing in the slaty austere sea.

BLACK LIGHT

Having swum for seven
years in a foreign language,
I have decided to write
its dictionary down, out, word for word,
and illustrate the text with negatives.
One by one I hold them
up to the inner window.
Careful: these pictures speak,
these words have edges felt
through heavy velvet gauntlets.
A ray of dust
cuts cleanly in through the windows.
Simple and pure as mud, the years drip off.

Sky: ink. Sea: milk.
That Christmas noon around the café table:
under a striped awning
white eye-slits, white lip-slashes
make faces.

I white out one or two
halos and proceed
to turn a new leaf over.
But wait. First shut my eyes.

Translation of the pallor of that time
(I'd always missed the point):
the sky was black!
Crosshatched illuminations,
chiaroscuro gleaming neon—

details etched in dry point—
to see in a new light,
bathe in the gaze's acids,
then pull dripping from the eye's deep well.
Eyes that peel the past's
fat off—or zip each layer of dialect
down to its body-stocking, simple babble . . .
I see a crusty palimpsest held up.
Chalk dust and pencil shavings are brushed off.
Then the purplish black
blubber diving suit
peels into stinging air.
Fresh as a Xerox, the wincing bones step forth.

That wine-dark sea has bleached to fine chablis.
Tingling, it yields transparent
secrets to my throat.

FLYING HOME

Down milk-bright colonnades
the leper's bell recedes.

Shades lowered against the gleaming waste of ice,
I sit back, bathe in lukewarm acquiescence.

Dutiful, prompt,
strapped, doped, a little drunk,

squinting at international afternoon
I'll soon pass GO again.

And if these colored pencils, nose drops, passport
should plummet with the rest of the huge oval,

giant time capsule soft for the shark's maw,
will a notebook ambered back to front with words

rescue me from oblivion?
Syrup of skittish travelers, fame. I yawn.

WISH GRANTED

You said "I will go to another land, I will go to another sea. "
—Cavafy

Far city, agora and games and temple
seen clear and whole only from this distance,
what figure threads your gleaming maze
foreshortened in strong sunlight?

In the guise of an office worker
I took a bus back to the coast each evening.
Darkness rose from the Royal Gardens
lit in flares by peanut vendors' fires;
couples spooned in the gloom;
gardeners resembled monkeys under palm trees.

Now the mask falls.
Cloud shadows mark these hills.
Green, green;
back in the tree land I want sea again.

In any landscape you will be the same,
life size, a woman using this place up.
You say you're tired of azure skies?
So be it.

     Roll of thunder!
Subaqueous light. Racing over a hayfield
you skid on wet grass, kick the bales downhill.
It may not all get in before the sky cracks.
Over a dead elm, lightning!
Wide sweet cool smell after weeks of drought.

It is not the rain, it is the idea of home.
Let it end here if it has to,
the pattern be lopped off with one hot jolt,
scorching silence,
and the wide hayfield tilting.

TRIPTYCH

Flanked by the yes and no
mirroring opposites,
encounter and refusal,
the central cameo:

my own unfolding body—
bloodless, aglow like wine.
The bird/heart now weighs in.
Head under coded wing,

all downy damp potential
to fly away? to sing?
to be? to beat? Remain
aorist, dear icon,

precious as captured time
and real as wind and rain.

MAKING SENSE OF SALT WATER

Try to see landscape whole and one wrong tree
marks out a hemisphere and spoils the view.
But near the ocean things obligingly
dilute into a noncommittal blue
matrix against which figures stand out sharply,
including me and you.

Like every island, this one's rich with runes
to spell a story out in weed, in water.
In turn we recapitulate the moon's
rhythmical tide-tug. We lie down, two stones
bared on the beach, or gull-like mew and veer,
flap heavily through sea-fog's long cocoons.

The tide flows
outward, washes back,
leaves clues behind
in a salt alphabet. No final answer.
These hazy days each time the sun goes under,
houses and boats are drained again of color,
smeared by the old confusion: sky with sea,
one coastline, island, ocean with another.
A new confusion pours you into me.

It hurts the eyes, I know, that milky glare
rising from nowhere. Still, stay near a shore.
In time we shall discover
another island, many islands, crowning from black water,
rolled between the maker's thumb and finger
out of chewy air.

FIVE DISGUISES

Deliberate footsteps braid
   a strand from room to room.
      Crossing the gloom
  she balances a vessel on her head
whose hidden contents nobody may know.
    Whatever deadly water
       bubbles and winks and threatens to slop over,
   no spill, no stain may mar
the glossy dark perfection of the floor.

I see you bear it too,
   cargo so breakable
      you must stand quite still.
   It may expand and fill you to your toes
or shrink until it's tiny—but it stays,
   gauging heat and fever.
     It mounts like mercury to measure anger
   and sometimes grows so tall
within you that you stagger, almost fall.

Curving along the sand,
   look! they have built a thick
     high wall of brick
  to separate the ocean from the land.
But if a tidal wave should rear its tower
   from that flat satin sea,
     the sturdy wall would crumble in a high
   advancing mound of water,
all elements smashed violently together.

Chronic, obscure, a pain
    in pockets of your life
        demands a knife
    at last. You lance the wound to make it drain,
sacrifice smoothness, scar the perfect skin,
    and feel it turning mild,
        the hurt you've nurtured since you were a child.
    Naked and strange,
to shuffle the old ailment off; to change.

The closet's full of clutter.
    What have I come to find?
        Ah yes. Behind
    a pile of ancient costumes I discover
the mask I used to wear over what was
    not quite a finished face.
        It pressed the features firmly into place.
    Habit by now alone
strong as a mask can mold the tender bone.

PANTOUM ON PUMPKIN HILL

The goldenrod sheds pollen in the butter.
The lawn mower, just before it stops, goes sputter.
The valleys echo roars from the wood cutter.
I write a word down; mouth it; finally utter.

The lawn mower, just before it stops, goes sputter.
My mother sinks to sleep with gentle snores.
I write a word down; mouth it; finally utter.
Quiet is sifting in from out of doors.

My mother sinks to sleep with gentle snores.
The typewriter cricket clicks its code.
Quiet is sifting in from out of doors.
The white cat pounces at a tardy toad.

The typewriter cricket clicks its code.
Upstairs you pace, you halt, you mark out time.
The white cat pounces at a tardy toad.
I chew a fingernail and find a rhyme.

Upstairs you pace, you halt, you mark out time.
Stand on the balcony, survivors; stare
(I chew a fingernail and find a rhyme)
at something time has no more terrors for.

Stand on the balcony, survivors; stare.
Never before have I dug quite so deep
at something time has no more terrors for
beyond the honeyed film of summer sleep.

Never before have I dug quite so deep.
The world is fragile, old, and very small
beyond the honeyed film of summer sleep
I follow syllable by syllable.

The world is fragile, old, and very small.
We've shrunk to dolls, our rhetoric's a mutter
I follow syllable by syllable:
the goldenrod sheds pollen in the butter.

from **A Son from Sleep** (1987)

CODEX MINOR

The headless bird flew back
to the winter root, its tree.
Strong red clay and bones:
stuff my foreign songs
sprang from, not understood
till now, nor now, but hard
against the tongue, the brain—
this late-returning pain
comes surely home to roost.

The village spoke and said:
Your roots are steeped in red,
your bones are benches, mugs,
a shawl, a hut, a tank,
a densely carved-on tree.
Think back to splintered wood.
No name, no family.
The tale not fully grown,
stories not understood.

What does it mean, this late-
night life, ungathered, turning?
Tardy recognitions in the dark?
The blood-red bird flies back to me and says:
Your roots are soaked in red.
I have no song, bird. Make the words for me.
Here is the body; you possess the head.
Escape but find my elemental tree.
Water the roots, blind groper; mouth and spout
beyond all hope of pushing in or out.

The beach in Ormos, then. A single gull
suspended in the air; a porcelain
brilliance; a limpidity; no motion
except Andreas and his son
were working with their hands
in wood. On wood. A boat. A big caique.
They kissed a little cross
and propped it on the prow
and—gently, slowly—set the thing in motion.
I looked up at the sky again with knowledge.
Could I come here again, I said, to live?
Could I come here again?

IN LIEU OF A LULLABY

> Sleep, sleep, happy sleep,
> While o'er thee thy mother weep.
> —Blake, "Cradle Song"

What you are sucking is my life till now,
griefs, pleasures, weathers; all the nights and days
distilled, then watered down to drinkable
blandness you unhesitatingly

turn to, take in. My nipples sometimes sting
or ache, are tired of your thirsty tugging,
and sometimes thirst for you.
I fed my own old face until you came.

When you weep it is not yet with real tears.
I do not know your language yet. These bodies
cling together, share a root of life.
And what I weep for isn't broken sleep,

dreamless; or years of broken nights ahead;
it isn't for the broad unanchored wake
of years and seasons and indulgences
that gleams and rolls behind me;

nor even that for half a sunlit life
I feared and waited. Not
this, or not only this; whatever might have happened,
it would not have been you

as you are now, here, bumping at my neck,
or cuddling in the corner of the crib.
No. What makes me weep,
awful, automatic as a faucet,

is simply singing you
my pitiful small stock of lullabies.
Hush Little Baby; Go Tell Aunt Rhodie;
Rock-a-bye Baby—one and all turn out

to be such litanies of infant loss,
disaster rediscovered, hummed in tunes
that turn my faded memories of babyhood
green and in a twinkling

wet. What isn't wet these days? Tears, blood,
crap, pee, night sweats, dissolving down to new
core, bone to milk: the strangeness, day by day.
You suck this salt

in with the milk, or do you?
Before your birth I feared you'd soak in fears
I croon tonight in words
some other mother once upon a time

made, and other mothers,
loving and fearing, sang, and still are singing:
And if that horse and cart fall down,
You'll still be the sweetest little baby in town.

LYING UNDER A QUILT

Twilight: a drowsy dim
haven of thick repose
and half the journey done,
we sleepily suppose.
Hidden in either self,
memories lodge in lips,
creased into secret cells;
we're quiet, touching hips,

lying under a quilt,
catted on either flank,
our little boy asleep
on the other side of the wall,
and summer still ungroomed,
bugs in the bushy grass,
rain hanging undecided
whether or not to fall.

I see you—shining islands
haloed with sheer desire!
Unearthly mauve and crimson
sculptings of upper air!
I swoop, I solo float,
I sacrifice it all
for color beyond thought,
gesture, ineffable!

Through empyrean brilliance
our son is cast, a shadow
growing up exiled, empty
of what no one but me
or you can give him. You.

You too were left behind!
My arms are empty. Flailing
I thrash, make up my mind,
clip the wide-flung wings
and fall down the bright air
which speaks to me in light:
Come dive me, plunge me, here.
My purifying fire
gilds all you hope to be,
to travel, to discover,
and everything you've done.

        Again my breast
hardens. Milk comes down.
As constant dripping wears away a stone
so I am hard and softened, bottleful
of riches, magical
and always out of reach
till need uncorks me. Gently,
then, the contents leach.

ODE ON HIS SLEEP

Each time I check your succulent
   sleep you have once again
done your nocturnal spin,
   completely changed position.
Spread-eagled on your lambskin with one toe
   halfway out the window
or hunched with rump in air are only two
   points of a compass that points everywhere.

Plump duckling, each new day like each new food
   you take serenely in, and hungrily
assimilate and make yourself the more.
   What you don't need you easily excrete.
You shake each new day's troubles off your back.
   Desiring you tiny once again,
tucked safely into sleep, is only my
   provisioning for what I know I'll lack.

The chubby fist poked out between the bars,
   the foot half numb with sleep,
the mouth half open and its sweet low breath:
   so many separate stars
I want to join together with one line
   and shape an infant constellation
twinkling above the babies in the lane.
   Immortalize you. There's a consolation.

At night your father, you, and I are slung
   in individual hammocks through the black
loom of a jungle restlessly patrolled
   by native roaches, silently. Asleep,
we're each of us enmeshed
   in hours of wordless breath.
Awake, I seem to see us all as shapes
   in darkness, both up close

and also as if from an enormous distance.
    I see we're born to shake the bars, outgrow
the crib, and toddle off—fast lane or slow
    comes to one end. We shake our limbs in love
a little while. Years push us on and on.
    Tired, we are glad to see the cozy pen,
its tidy lines dividing time and space again.
    We climb back in and sleep a lifetime off.

TWO AND ONE

Asleep between us
(father, mother
pushing a stroller)
this treasure is.

Gain from loss.
Good-bye, speech;
here in reach
is Paradise—

here in the park,
the dogs, the dirt,
my milky shirt,
cries in the dark.

Was all along?
Yes and no.
Until I had you
I had it wrong.

The focus given—
an infant's face—
they are one place,
hell and heaven.

We lose to find.
Youth, beauty,
wave good-bye.
I bend my mind,

strike my temple,
try to grapple
with the riddle,
yet it's simple:

Janus-face,
here you are.
You light up space
like a single star.

On either side
an emptiness—
here Born, there Died—
fills the place

yet fades away
in the glow
of a single day.
I know, I know:

you weren't always here.
And you'll go. (When?)
You'll disappear.
Birth/death: twin

mirrors reflecting
only each other
over the sleeping
head in the stroller

lose their power,
pale in one
brilliant hour
of living sun.

Brush of a wing—
or is it blade?—
flickering
over what we've made,

that angel love,
enormous knife,
wing of a dove
scoring life

swoops its shadow
invisibly
into a meadow
where we three,

mother, father,
baby, lie
close together
under the sky.

Trees are in flower.
Grass is green.
The hour is noon
and is forever.

from **Pass It On** (1989)

HOW CAN I PUT YOU DOWN?

(from "The Fields of Sleep")

How can I put you down?

Nightly you must negotiate alone
fluorescent escalators, straddle
banisters gleaming neon
and noiselessly slide down.

How can I tell you "sleep"?

Nightly the body yearns to recreate
its lost polarity,
shape of love unsculpted,
lost or forgotten mate.

How can I let you cry?

Nightly you must move on
toward that point where all roads come
together into one
lost just as it touches the horizon.

How can I shut the door?

Nightly you must go through
so many dark arcades
and come back whole
clutching morning's clue.

SUNDAY MORNING

(from "The Fields of Sleep")

Sunday morning. Smell of something dead
rises through boards of the porch
floor where mother and son
sit dragging loaded brushes over newsprint.
Patches of red and orange wait for meaning
to dry. What lies below
rots at a sultry pace;
what lives takes shape and nods,
sleepy with summer, stubbornly still growing.

Her finger pricked, the Sleeping Beauty fell
asleep for a hundred summers
as a result of which (the child
dabbing the spindle red
adds) she felt much better.

I LEAN MY LADDER

(from "Fix It")

I lean my ladder on
the beautiful, the flawed
handiwork of God
and turn to spy my son

busy way down there
patching a balloon,
filling in the moon.
The whole world needs repair.

Broken! he calls the moon
if it is less than round—
syllables that resound
domestically soon,

as light bulb, pencil, tile
get broken. His decree
Fix it! shows faith in me
that prompts me first to smile

and then suppress a sigh
and fetching tape and glue
climb up to mend the blue
disasters in the sky.

I lean my ladder on
the beautiful, the flawed
handiwork of God
and turn to spy my son.

HORTUS CONCLUSUS

to Mark and Sam Rudman

Our walk that Sunday in the mind's kind eye
has mellowed to unmitigated good
(not that from the start there wasn't joy)
like so many days of parenthood.
Days? Hours. Hour. Each bestrollered son
(Jonathan at two and Sam at one)
inaugurates the day by eating jam
cookies at the Hungarian patisserie
across from the Cathedral, while you
and I share cappuccino to go,

which I can savor two months later—now.
Can see the leashed white rabbit on the lawn
nibbling while petted, just a step or two
from the huge, ecumenical, brand new
Cathedral fountain's statue. Step back! We
need to decode this iconography.
Two praying hands, two Pegasus-like wings;
crab claws; twined flowers; a great smiling face
of sun or moon, if the moon has rays;
and at the top, scaling a horn of plenty,
androgynous Andromeda or saint,
a rescued maiden reaches for the sky.
However overloadedly baroque,
somehow the sense is of serenity,
as what is not, seen from not too close up?

Let's move on. The boys already have,
lacking, so far, a taste for allegory.
Besides, the unfinished fountain is still dry.

Where have they vanished? We both start to run.
Sam's among bushes, chasing a red hen.
Jonathan, standing in a patch of sun,
intercepts crusts of bread a shirtless man
(monk, beggar, saint?) smilingly scatters to
the birds, the boys—all's one. A flash of blue
illuminates the underbrush. Boys, look!
It isn't every day you see a peacock!
See how it struts and preens and juts its head!
All right, don't look. You're hungry; have some bread.
Remember jam from half an hour ago
still smearing your four ruddy cheeks? No? No.

Further from the fountain, a green wall
hides a secret: the enclosed and small
garden whose every plant is biblical.
Luckily this scrawny quince tree shows
no fruit, as yet, to pluck. Two ladies knit
on a stone bench—the same bench where I sat
in early June not quite three years ago
wondering whether the blood test would show
what I already knew or thought I knew . . .

a memory I might have time to blurt
to you, but Sam starts howling. Is he hurt?
("Sam's crying," Jonathan puts in his two
cents' worth of sober realism to you.)
No, only tired. Heavy-eyed, napward bound,
breaded and jammed, both settle back without a sound,
each in his deck chair taking in the scene,
two tiny passengers finally headed home.

Over the strollers you and I begin
to gather the loose edges up again
of the diffuse long dialogue that we
seem to sustain, however interruptedly,
the gaps and eddies of poetic logic
garbled by two, three, four, six lives' pace
but leapfrogged over by our friendship's magic.
Admittedly most of our talk these days
sounds simply like complaint. I kvetch to you
about the things you kvetch about to me.
With unrehearsed simultaneity
we talk about the damages of time,
how spring feels done and summer coming on.
Trudging home, we trample over rhyme,
vision, perfection, what's impossible
or wishable to try for. Resonance
of acts or names—as parent, poet, teacher—
we both have blindly struggled to attain.

We talk about the blossoming of speech,
substantives learned, subjunctive within reach,
and future beckoning. We even toss
out into sunlight a black label: loss.
Not daily chaos, insufficient sleep;
I meant more. I meant that when we grow
up into the world is when we start
to wish—no, not to wish—well, to let go.
Each child does its little flaxen bit
to pry us loose, and we begin to die.

The sun's now at the zenith in the sky
above us. In this dance there is no way
to clasp hands with the dead and living equally.
The quick, the dead change places as they can
(do your two half-dead fathers make up one live man?).
Beyond the consolation of our back
and forth, we cast a glance
over our shoulders at the dream
creature rising from the raw
fountain of hope, its waters not yet flowing.
We remember the improbable peacock,
the rabbit unconcernedly
nibbling outside the secret garden. Look:
a new moon bobbing on its length of string
over the broken world. And I remember
however deciduous the two
of us may feel, it's spring.
This morning's jaunt—not even half a day,
measured in clock time—was our fumbling way
to celebrate a season which may well
never feel new to us again. No matter.
The boys (both now asleep) deserved an hour,
a day, an instant—oh, the hell with time—
a memory of rabbit, peacock, sun,
statue, jam, or rooster—all by now
receding in a sentimental glow
to the rosy, the unblemished good
one sees (it's pure illusion, God knows how)
when looking back at days of parenthood.

PASS IT ON, I

Like a huge tree house out of mortal reach,
high platforms thickest foliage nearly hides.
Instead of speech,
hands reach across and down to help us up.
Translation: crossing over the abyss,
handing the little ones, the old ones over
to who'll receive them. Carryings
from here to the invisible and endless.
Tradition: handing on and handing down
and handing up, a laying on of hands.
Hand over hand pass on, press in
the secret of ascent:
gravity's up. The jungle is too lush
to walk in, so we all find other ways
of navigating: flail, wade, bracchiate,
hooting like happy apes,
or silently, staggeringly, smoothly
swim, angels, fishes, forward through the green
gloom towards a height, a waterfall
or treefall one can climb? A gap; a dome;
more reaching hands; and a pervasive light.

PASS IT ON, II

I grope to find the phrases for two thoughts.
One, everything is new—
butterfly   doorknob   toothbrush
        clap your hands
look at the light   the light

and two, I'm starting to run out of words
for private use. You'd think
that one could give and keep at the same time,
        take through giving,
twin gestures, teaching/mothering: two tasks

you give your blood and brains to and they thank you
by passing plates for more. Okay, okay,
I didn't do it to be thanked. And yet
        the bottom of the barrel
feels perilously close to glinting up.

Crusty tongue. Cups that once held milk.
A mouth begins as organ of ingestion,
then gets its teeth in talk and never stops.
        Cup breast tongue
all provided courtesy of mother.

I never thought of thanking mine for years.
She never made those velvet vocables,
smooth secret treasures, taffy to the palate,
        mine to keep,
in fact my own invention, I knew,

not some old heirloom. Later I let go.
They fell from my open mouth and I live on
to tell the tale again.
        Pass it on.
Keep words and eat them. Don't your eyes light up

equally at "cookie" or any other noun
you recognize?—all goodies you'll hand down,
as the phrase goes, we hope, to your own children.
   A body passes
through a body, changing it forever.

Carry on the torch was what they told me
in high school, i.e. teach; be like your father.
Knowledge, it seemed, was like a relay race.
   I didn't know
the torch would have to pass through my own body.

TEACHING EMILY DICKINSON

What starts as one more Monday morning class
merges to a collective Dickinson,
separate vessels pooling some huge truth
sampled bit by bit by each of us.

She sings the pain of loneliness for one.
Another sees a life of wasted youth;
then one long flinching from what lay beneath
green earth; last, pallid peerings at the stone

she too now knows the secret of.

                        Alone,
together, we'd decipher BIRD SOUL BEE
dialect humdrum only until heard
with the rapt nervy patience, Emily,
you showed us that we owed you. One small bird
opens its wings. They spread. They cover us:
myriad lives foreshortened into Word.

PASS IT ON, III

Lilacs look neon in fading light.
Death makes life shine:
a tiredness, a flickering between

ages, which is each age;
a piling up to tottering
and falling back to sand.

So much for cycle. The front door lock
sticks each fall when we're first back.
We are advised to oil it.

Olive oil in the keyhole:
again the old key turns.
Once again to meander

along the edge of water,
whether tideless sea or tidal river,
pushing the stroller, dreaming

oil in the lock; the key
dipped in lubricity
the boychild's shining skin
me tired to the bone

Already summer's over.
Goodbye, lilacs. Your
neon is past; you'll bloom again

next spring. Past an age
each season feels like an end of summer
but still the tale's to tell

over and over for those
lolling and snoozing in the stroller,
preparing to come after.

Tall house standing on its high green hill—
children, do you remember?
Lawns slant down to a stream.

Under a striped tent
a buffet's spread in the sun.
Ideas of the eternal,

once molten, harden; cool.
Oil, oil in the lock.
The old key turns.

TEACHING THE ILIAD

Teaching the text, I feel
the little hairs along my forearms rise
and shield my eyes
against the nimble letters on the page.
They spell a man
who weeps and weeps alone
for his brief golden age.
Presently the line where sea meets sky
fills with silhouetted men. An army
deployed behind him comes between
margin and horizon like a screen
on which hexameters drum down like rain.

GENERATIONS

I

How well I understand it now, my father's
dumbshow pointing, tragicomic reaching
for salt or butter. Too much trouble to
find the words for whatsitsname when your
anonymous familiars know your needs.
No need of endless labels. Today the baby
points to my shoe, says *Mama's—*
articulating that apostrophe.
He calls for ham and raisins, not because
he wants them, though he does. Rather it's that
the words wait, shining virgins, for his use.

II

Bathroom scale, thermometer are *ock*
for clock. And *ock* is also hot; block; box; socks.
Nin means pin, *ninny* for short, and *nen*
means pen or pencil. *Gok*: dog. *Guk*: milk.
Mama and Daddy are self-evident
and Grandma has no name and then is Amma.
Aisin: raisin. *Asses*: glasses. *Io*: cheerio.
Bubble is bubble, whether blown in play,
or drops of water in the bath, or bits
of dandelion fluff that, puffed at, blow away.

III

So as he picks up language's far-shadowing
spear and brandishes it recklessly,
I'm sinking mildly into the resigned
dumbness of middle age. Had known some such
chiasmus would be coming, but so fast!

Pale and solemn, shadowed by the tent's
lurid red and yellow stripes, he rides
the carousel at the Kiwanis Carnival
around and around. Perched on the neighboring horse
sidesaddle, I just manage not to touch
his hands that tightly clutch the pole. His head.

IV

Some experts find the fear of nuclear
annihilation foremost in the minds
of children; others claim that we project
our terrors onto their unconsciousness,
the true concerns of kids being narcissistic.
Why shouldn't both be right? We live in hell,
preferring not to dwell too morbidly
on our condition. Double-natured, we
thirst for the ease of dream and fable, food
and mirror, money, ivory, and horn.

V

Focusing on zero, you look
at it and at it and finally through it
and see a tiny chiseled nameless thing
lying at the bottom of a well
or anywhere sky and water meet.
Then sky turns dark and smoky.
A thin black line stretches from end to end
for us to dance across
from pole to pole, believing, not believing,
having no choice but to entrust ourselves
to the torqued embrace of twin impossibles.

VI

After the Chinese food and beer and kisses of reunion,
sleepily we talk of death and birth,
of terror and of comfort, their equation:
grandmother dying of cancer,
baby astir in the womb.
A cockroach crawls in the beer mug.
The cat with the ulcered ear
purring reaches up a paw to knead
the beard of the father-to-be
who soon will dive from his fragile tower
into an unfathomed blood-warm sea.

VII

We sit and cogitate our common lot,
each of us remembering, foreseeing
those deaths we know the best. Outlined, macabre,
the sonogrammed infant seems to shake her fist.
And in the chic boutique you've told me of,
a teddy bear winds up to white womb noises—
amnio growls to soothe the savage breast
of a new creature thrust bald and wild
into such a strangely silent world.
Latest in lullabies, bubble and squeak
of guts, lub-dub of the maternal heart.

VIII

Scattered in play over the lawn, these beans
(*neens*, says the baby) oddly root and tangle
in the matted turf. Not odd—stubborn.
They want to live. And lovely fragile poppies,
great petals tousled by one day of rain,
droop in the shaggy border.
But I was thinking of the beans—
inscrutable containers, possibilities

by the handful (one was black, one white),
popping in grass and in my head at night,
crammed with meaning, coded for the future.

IX

Toddler in nursing home, cooings predicted—
so weak the link between imagination and event.
Two caged lovebirds chitter and flirt in the lobby
(bronze; marble; mirrors; the only mirrors here).
Upstairs he does look, smile, say "Amma"; then
dashes immediately from the room
into the hall. Explore! Patrol! Discover
for whom that goll keeps tolling (goll = bell).
They may have shared some signs of recognition
unequally. She can't reach out to him;
sheer quicksilver, he cannot sit still.

X

Flies in amber? Something viscous, heavy,
transparent, gradually hardens
around them, slows them down
at last to utter immobility.
Those who still live must struggle to wade through it,
totter (Time's stilts, said Proust). No energy
to spare for signs of recognition. Only
a few, incarcerated by mistake,
claw at the translucent envelope.
You and I, younger, move more freely through
our thickening matrix. Naked, the baby flies.

FIRST NIGHT BACK

Back in the country, too
    happy to fall asleep
this first night. Buried summers
    keep me up.

An all-embracing web
    threaded from room to room—
memory looping myth—
    touches not me alone

but all who breathe here, sigh,
    sleep, remember, dream.
Is that a monstrous bat
    bumping against the screen?

If I commit myself
    to turning out the light,
the panicky bump-bump
    will relocate

inside my skull. Too
    happy here to fall
asleep, my jackknifed friend,
    or not at all

happy? These words are two
    sides of a single coin
flipping itself for hours
    in my old room.

Simply being alive
    is keeping me awake.
If sleep's a little death,
    why dive into the dark?

Opposites baffle me.
    The country's what is real.
Here's where I drive a car,
    put hands in soil;

and nothing here seems real.
    It all accumulates
grotesquely: mason jars,
    memories, straw hats,

tins of dried-up tea,
    shells from some dry sea . . .
Just to unpack means raising thick
    clouds of *nostalgie*.

Everything's gone beyond
    limits. The trees have grown
far past the planter's purpose. Deep
    shadows stripe the lawn.

Finally everything
    will fall apart, corrupt,
dear bodies sifting back to soil;
    but that keeps me awake

too! As we age and age,
    I like to catch us at it.
May no natural change for me
    ever seem automatic.

The blossoming of trees,
    lilacs late into May—
it takes me hours of moonlight
    to understand one day,

the first day of our summer.
    Our son's first summer here
shoots him up to boldness
    and down to sheer

frustration. Doorknobs; stairs;
  grass higher than his head;
great ants; a rake; a trowel;
  bare feet on a dirt road;

flowers to warm his hands at;
  lunches of bread and jam;
he doesn't say *I'm happy.*
  He lives *I am*

all day. All day, all night
  in my childhood's room
we wear our bodies deeper
  and deeper into time.

THREE SILENCES

I

Of all the times when not to speak is best,
mother's and infant's is the easiest,
the milky mouth still warm against her breast.

Before a single year has passed, he's well
along the way: language has cast its spell.
Each thing he sees now has a tale to tell.

A wide expanse of water = ocean. Look!
Next time, it seems that water is a brook.
The world's loose leaves, bound up into a book.

II

The habit holds for love. He wants to seize
lungsful of ardent new sublimities.
Years gradually pry him loose from these.

He comes to prize a glance's eloquence,
learning to construct a whole romance
from hint and gesture, meaning carved from chance.

And finally silence. Nothing in a phrase
so speaks of love as an averted gaze,
sonnets succumbing to remembrances.

III

At the Kiwanis traveling carnival
I ride beside you on the carousel.
You hold on solemnly, a little pale.

I don't stretch out my hand. You ride alone.
Each mother's glance reduplicates my own:
the baffled arc, the vulnerable bone.

Myself revolving in the mirror's eye
as we go round beneath a cloudy sky,
eying my little boy attentively,

I swallow what I was about to say
(no loving admonition is the way
to bridge this gap) and hear the music play

and later, wordless, reach and lift you down
over the rigid horse's shiny brown
mane, and press your body close against my own.

Stillness after motion,
the creaky music cranking, cranking down,
the carnival preparing to leave town.

THE END OF SUMMER

Sweet smell of phlox drifting across the lawn—
an early warning of the end of summer.
August is fading fast, and by September
the little purple flowers will all be gone.

Season, project, and vacation done.
One more year in everybody's life.
Add a notch to the old hunting knife
Time keeps testing with a horny thumb.

Over the summer months hung an unspoken
aura of urgency. In late July
galactic pulsings filled the midnight sky
like silent screaming, so that, strangely woken,

we looked at one another in the dark,
then at the milky magical debris
arcing across, dwarfing our meek mortality.
There were two ways to live: get on with work,

redeem the time, ignore the imminence
of cataclysm; or else take it slow,
be as tranquil as the neighbors' cow
we love to tickle through the barbed wire fence
(she paces through her days in massive innocence,
or, seeing green pastures, we imagine so).

In fact, not being cows, we have no choice.
Summer or winter, country, city, we
are prisoners from the start and automatically,
hemmed in, harangued by the one clamorous voice.

Not light but language shocks us out of sleep—
ideas of doom transformed to meteors
we translate back to portents of the wars
looming above the nervous watch we keep.

NOURISHMENT

Love—its long spoon, its promise, and its threat—
you won't go empty, I shall make you eat,
        I'll fend off death—
apostrophizes an averted face,
retreats with a reluctant backward glance.

Agitated wings
flap at the cold containment of the moon,
        fluttering
batlike, bewildered out of a dark cave
and bump themselves on light's solidity

as on an arm outstretched in utter trust,
patient as trees, pouring itself, until
        ethereal
it has been drained of every precious cell
to share with who may happen to be dry.

A house of appetite and sustenance
links, shelters, and divides
        inhabitants who feed,
work, walk together and as in a dream
undoing the loose bonds of need float free.

You and I, walking to this silent house,
encounter no warm gold
        ring of lantern light
such as draws chilly travelers and moths.
No lamp burns here but blood,

mortal fuel consumed at steady speed.
Ghosts in disappointment flit away,
        hunger unsatisfied.
Dim in the room we turn to one another,
open our lips, and speak

a single word and raise a mutual finger.
Into such stillness no new thing should spill,
        muddy the mirror
we turn our double back to speechlessly
and sit and eat our fill.

from **Living in Time** (1990)

WATER AND FIRE

To James Merrill

Water and fire and a beloved face
are magnets for the eye of memory.
Yet set against a span of evening sky
that canopies a lifetime's sacred space,
how perfidiously they seem to change!
Oceans divide. Love's features multiply.
Athens, Vermont, Aurora Borealis—
by their very halos, all are blurred.

So that this seeker of eternity,
finally forced to shut her eyes to the
beauties whose icons prove ephemeral,
turns, sighing, to your inexhaustible
books, which englobe lost worlds in every word.

INCUBATION

I came back to the island to lie down.
The dream machine suspended over the bed—
will it yield up a sign?
Each successive generation here
consults its proper oracle—fog, tide,
cloudy beach glass washed up on the shore.
My choice is incubation.
From the accumulated stock of dreams
I have decided to entrust myself
to faceless phantoms talking out of time;
to take the chances of the summer moon,
perpetually old, renewed, and clean;
to step back into an unlighted room
with bandaged eyes and look at the unseen.
The broad bed that receives me
has presided over so much sleep
it is imbued with dreams.
Clusters of them, invisible in daylight,
hang upside down like bats.
I yields to *we.*

If the whole island were to incubate,
could its collective vision become real?
Entire communities can dream as one.
Last winter in a place between two hills
a single bonfire reddened
empty hours before a snowy dawn.
Lovers grope down adjacent corridors
and find the chamber where they both began:
her anteroom of shadow memories
lit up as labyrinth for his avid tracing,
his childhood a dark hall that she explores.

But summer, islands are centrifugal.
"This place," says every islander I've known,
"would be a paradise without the people."
The custom of the country's to unload
each family's luggage from the ferryboat
in shrouded little nuggets, gold or grief,
toss it in separate wagons, haul it home,
always uphill and heavy, always hidden.
So many days the island hides itself.
Slugs slick paths and mist hangs from the trees.
The ocean's lovely lulling rhythms are
relentlessly impersonal. The tide
that washes over my beloved dead
is dragging your desires out to sea.
It pulls them back and slaps them at my feet.
Moon as we may at fog horns, do they give
a hoot for any human ecstasy?
Heartlike, they throb through murk, they mark the time;
at most they are a kind of metronome.
Life here is something private people live—

as if this island, spine to which one sails
rockingly over the astringency
of water's brilliance or opacity,
were free of all the tools that people use
to net a memory, fix a precious face,
screw an image firmly into place.
Happy families may be all alike
but houses differ here; each has its own
private version of the dream machine.
Unwritten and unsaid but understood,
the island grid clicks into place like law.
No huge machine is anchored at the cove
to climb into and float beyond the bay.
We shut our doors,
pull down the shades on a diminished love.

IN THE HAMMOCK

Starting with fairy tales, we swing,
these hazy summer days, from heroes' feats
down to the intricate workings of a blood cell
and back to songs that mermaids sing.
Galaxies unimaginably vast
born where space and time curl up together
(or is it that they die there?)
become just one more story of the past.

Together you and I
scan the enormous tome we may be near
the end of, stubbornly
seeking in chaos evidence of choice:
black hole, lightning, dinosaur, virus—chosen!
Your guiding clue is mine, a mother's voice.

MOMENTS OF SUMMER

The horizontal tugs me more and more.
Childhood hours spent reading with my father
rise in a kind procession once again.
Disparate gravities of our two ages
dissolve as we lie back and let the pages
take us, float us, sail us out to sea.

What special spell (not always narrative:
the winter we read *De Senectute*
I was fifteen; you had two years to live)
braided our endless differences to one?
Today a mother reading to my son,
I savor freshly that sweet nourishment,
especially if we are lying down.

ALWAYS AFTERNOON

You ask, this honeyed drop of summer time,
the creaking hammock as our pendulum,
what if the world were made of raspberries?
If sunny afternoons went on and on?

In the land of the Lotus Eaters
we're told that it was always
or at least "seemed always afternoon."
But Odysseus longed for the dawn of his return.

Achilles could discern his death approaching
guestlike at a particular time of day.
There will come, he said, a morning
or an afternoon or an evening.

Human desire sets memory like a clock
to a particular nick of crucial time
we wish to get to and then not look back
and at one age and stage live on and on.

Once he has hit on the idea, King Lear
plans to continue kneeling to Cordelia
for the foreseeable future, like a clockwork
pageant in the parade of ever after.

Only with agony can Philoctetes
bid goodbye to the timeless
island of pain he has to rip himself
bloodily loose from and begin to live.

Thoreau says "Morning is when dawn's in me."
So let this slowly swinging hammock be
our ceremony of always afternoon
even as the seasons slide inexorably on.

LOVE AND NEED

(from "The Dream Machine")

Love. When you don't want to go to sleep,
I sometimes say "But can't you feel our love,
Daddy's and mine for you? It's hovering,
it's flying round the room, invisible
but there." Invisibility won't do.
Indignantly you practice for bereavement,
shaping your vision of the mighty figure
life coyly flashes out at us as children,
withholding for the nonce the ripened model
of separation. And I think you're right:
if love incarnate bristles with confusion,
love as abstraction cannot do the trick.
The wings that shade your sleep and waft you dreams
belong to solid beings, named and faced,
under whose protection you let love
move away a little from the door,
its finger in the book to hold the place.
Solitude circumscribes you. You let go.

Is it a bond like necrophilia
that shackles, as the living to the dead,
love and silence? Down the corridor
of night's perspective dwindling, my voice
fades and is replaced by what your five
years among us have left you with so far—
in other words, a formidable array
of memories, anecdotes, fears, fantasies.
The dream machine, processing every place
you've ever lived in, cunningly condenses
garden, porch, stairway, corridor into one
Ur-dwelling where anything can happen.
Earthquakes, volcanoes, viruses, and witches
converge also into a single menace
no less frightening for being un-

visualizable—at least by me.
If shapeless terrors chill the hours of night,
what lights and heats an empty house? What voice
tells stories after I have left the room
you are a child in, fills the space to come?

In many ways mine was a fortunate
childhood. Yet I missed, and miss, that voice.
These lines are strung across a span of stillness.
For I can say it now:
some of what shaped me was a submerged struggle
stubbornly flickering on and off for years
against a silence I interpreted
as blankness, as indifference. Was I wrong?
Think of an aspiring puppeteer
whose medium is shadow. She cannot
project her figures onto wall or sheet
so long as no illumination
creates a magic screen where sharp black shapes
posture and cavort and entertain.
Rather a wan diffusion of light,
although it was dependable as bread,
seemed like a counsel of discouragement.
Nothing could ruffle the maternal stillness
flattening my furors, arguments,
confessions into chitchat. Into dumbness.
Love clothed as absence brooding in a room,
invisible, attentive, I immediately
recognize. When a beloved person
vanishes, the voice that's left behind
imprinted on our innermost attention
lingers far longer than the body's motion.
We see or think we see a moving figure
hesitant an instant on the threshold;
we hear or think we hear a dear arrival,
car in the road rustling to a halt,
key of return whispering in the lock.

But these are empty visitations,
reflections of our desolate desires;
not emanations of the precious essence
that's what is left to us beyond the body
and that survives in language.
What prompts me to write all this to a son
who hasn't learned to read yet, who may well
never read this, but my instinctive trust
that in the kaleidoscope of time
speech struggles from its background and stands out
so sharply that its shards can still draw blood?

from **Unending Dialogue** (1991)

TAKING SIDES

Who wouldn't want to be elsewhere?
Afternoons I for one
would love to take a siesta.
And if the dream of horizontality
floats me off like a boat,
what tugs you two away I can imagine.
Nevertheless we're here,
students doodling at life's
dull and incessant lecture.

Our task today: to write against the clock.
Hush. The makework pastime
deepens to divination as we sit.
Can you make out the mortal
combat between twin wishes,
opposing poles of dumbness and of speech?
Each wants to win our trio
to his own way of thinking.
They hiss at us *"This is for your own good!"*

Dumbness desires the paper to stay white.
Language longs for dumbness
to open his mouth for once
and spill out the accumulated poison
into the tank of air,
into the bath of hours,
into the somber parody of a classroom
where we three bend our heads
and scribble away for life.

ELEGY VARIATIONS

I

Tears in themselves are not a test of love.
Call them the weeping, as a sore can weep,
of some fresh loss. They also signify
the precious rising sap of memory.
They water the green region of a smile.
They help to navigate the caves of ice
and float us through dim arches to a place
where pairs of mourners in the smoky air
lean toward each other as if their desire
were one unfolding for eternity.
No: the embrace
of shadow flesh is an embodiment
we come to late as we approach
that shore, our sluggish senses
thickening even as they seem to stretch.
Mourners, but mourners who must stay in motion,
we tip out tears, libations in the dust,
a few dark drops for the road,
and turn to trace the paths of separation.

II

I knew no better than to say "Don't cry"
to your "I love you" as we said goodbye.

Stubbornness and mercy of the earth!
Instinctively affections reattach
their hopeful suckers as the spring returns.
Spring pierces this pale room, so many blades
of light between the blinds.
I could have said "I've never trusted sun

in March; this year it's extra treacherous."
I hadn't come to talk about the weather.
To be there was to have entered a procession
halted as frieze. You in the center; M.
on one side held your hand; I on the other
stroked your long legs, touched your big right foot,
still calloused from your work, still flexed for more
dancing; apart, one shoulder to the wall,
your father, standing closest to the door.

Our places taken, not much need to speak.
Belatedly the flaws of winter break.

III

The letters smear the sky,
are scrawled over the gates.
No ambiguity:
they spell out IRON AGE.

But black winds bleed to white.
Sleep spreads the floor like fleece.
Who wades across this threshold
enters forgetfulness.

Echo, hour, echo:
gongs tremble, speak,
finally awaking memories
even in those who lack

reckoning. Take me—
I grope for where you are.
Yet your loss whisks the dust sheet
off my heart's desire.

Now I recall the quiet
deep waters of your will;
I see the garish sunlight
glazing the gritty sill.

Gallant at your going
you held yourself upright,
tilted toward what you said
goodbye to: light.

Tell me, was it despair
that spoke in a frozen voice,
or did the voice of winter
disguise itself as love?

THE REVENANT

A strange particularity
shapes this man asleep
beside me, whose least curve
I thought I knew by heart,
knew in my bones, knew inside
out (Greeks say *ap'exo*,
from outside in). But no:
the pulled-up knees and slender
ankles of a dead dancer
animate the dreaming
tenant of his body.
From near, from far
ghost and guest converge
to one form so familiar
it leaves love open
wide to forgery—
to the illusion that it doesn't matter
whose long-backed grace
is folded between these sheets,
what person, incognito,
either masked in blankness
or curled to fit the contour
of a former self
shares my bed. It's no
illusion life and death
are intertwined as any loving sleepers.
To be so beloved
must he not be familiar?
Fondly familiarity
breeds blindness: recognition
comes to be lodged
in loving touch alone.
I shut my eyes,
pass my fingertips
over the body
of the nameless breather.

LESS THAN KIND

SYPHILIS SURGE AND CRACK USE RAISE AIDS FEARS
Headline half gibberish, half storm at sea.
Escaping public weather, I retreat
to the remotest corner of the lawn.
And what do I tote to the hammock as my tutor?
Facts I thirst for, history as atrocity,
syphilis surge and crack or worse than these.
Fear, hunger, war, plague, death camp:
formerly herded under some umbrella
epithet like "inconceivable,"
the host of demons doesn't seem so strange
to me now swinging, reading
of them with more than simple recognition,
with—yes—a kind of longing.

Anatomize this leaning toward the crack
and surge, this almost putting out a hand.
Driven to articulate
abstraction into faces we might make,
we read our kind. The kinship's dim but deep.
More than curiosity, not quite memory,
but as a language newly learned uncovers
glassy blocks that shape a pyramid,
its shining structure inch by inch revealed,
so piece by piece the bad
news takes shape and is not
surprising; was always there;
was necessary to know.
Or just the fascination
that moves a child to study hurricanes,
earthquakes, tornadoes, twisters,
takes hold of us perusing our own pillage
scaled to human uses: RAISE AIDS FEARS
Metaphors we thought long dead take on
a phosphorescent half-life of their own:
raging illness expressed as rough sea,

verbs spume to nouns in general anarchy
emerging sleekly sea-changed: AIDS as death.
The nightmare mirror smashed to tiny shards
patiently pieced together through the long
eventless hours of a private summer:
finally a human
figure emerges, to a cry, if not
of triumph, of accomplishment
or recognition's perennial pleasure.

OCTOBER

October Thursdays. Circle of pale men
living their lives ahead of the unknown
allotted season, day, or afternoon,

hour, minute. (Achilles to Lykaon:
"Morning or midday, friend, my time will come.")
A waxy light pervades this basement room,

windowless; even so,
they always see as far as corridors
allow until a certain unmarked turn.

Lips twisted with Achilles' irony,
they straddle living bodies, tangled, warm;
they brush aside the doomed

ransom-bearer's feebly flourished gold.
Wait; it is themselves they wave away.
The bodies they bestride here are their own.

LAMENTS

Jenny Holzer installation, Dia Foundation, December 1989

Twilight seeps into this empty room,
garage, or attic, and the moon shines in.
Perched on a pew (this is the protocol),
one watches words stream past, a waterfall
beaded with light; then in the inner room
paces around the same words stuck in stone.
Too many messages come pouring in—
interrupted feasts, a trip by train—
though many slyly sheathe themselves in dreams
affectionate and kind and tinged with shame.
Sharing—that eucharistic fantasy
through which our isolated spirits try
to touch some surface shivering like skin . . .
As in a dream, the signs slide glittering past.
Their crucial message, both the first and last,
is "What we are is also what we see:
marble neon incessant elegy."

You and I once more prowl the inner room.
It's smaller; shedlike. History's dark barn
swept clean—are words the sweepings, or are we?
Does this whole faintly humming warehouse say
we've painted ourselves into a corner of
utterance? A long lament for love
finds its form first in inscription,
archive to epitaph to taph to tomb,
a recapitulation of our need
to set down phrases mourning our fresh dead.

Half sham-archaic Back to Basics, half
heroic unknown soldier's cenotaph;
logos or logo scribbled on the flat
affect of our postmodern habitat.
The letters whisk down; pause; start up once more.
Radical erasures flicker here.
Abstracted, next to you I sit, gaze, wait
for the electric shimmer to abate.
You say my eyes will get accustomed to
the dark; but since the symbols
keep pulsing to crescendo, guttering out,
sparking afresh the cool
stutter of silence, tape-loop troped as jewel,
nothing is constant, and they never do.

FIN DE SIECLE

Impossible to read a paragraph
these days and not to stumble over some
reference to imminent millennium—

sensation less of drowning than of draining.
Not one of us who wash around the sluice
but feels the suction. In a recent letter

F. writes of having "finally turned the corner
into the postmodern," and I picture
a brisk back being turned upon a life

left stranded on that corner ever after.
Future was once horizon; now it's angle
(Cavafy's angle to the universe,

said Forster). People also speak of cusps,
peaks, monstrous teeth or moons or mountain ranges.
Near you I sense no draining,

no corner turned, climacteric, finale,
no grandiose gesturings toward 2000.
It's January; and a few green leaves

shadow your light eyes like the hope of summer,
a picnic at the swimming hole, a walk
among wildflowers at the quarry's edge.

THE SLEEPING BEAUTY

Husk of a person beyond summer's pale,
the sleeping beauty dreaded to be woken
even by affection. The moon's veil
shrouded what little sky high monuments
(overgrown themselves by brambles) let
filter through. The spells had all been spoken.
Was it cruel or merciful to move
even a finger closer to the still
deeply breathing figure on the dais,
his slumber royal and illegible?

> Under layers of dust I glimpsed your face.
> As if our year of stories had alighted
> on those shut lips and would at the right word
> emerge and fly into the common air,
> I bent: to catch a signal? Steal a kiss
> never in the first place mine to take?
> Was I there to give or to receive?
> As soon as I approached, you seemed to stir,
> as who should ward off a too early waking.
> A pulse like hope beat blood into your cheeks.

The cornered moon sent grayish gleams of dim
illumination down—or transformation?
What would he do or say if he awoke?
Given new life, what would he become?
As I watched, the momentary motion
subsided, and the dream began again,
blanketing him for another year,
another hundred years, when he might wake
(sunlight and breakfast and the table set)
tuned to a kiss still drying on his lips—

> a kiss of friendship and the key to freedom,
> expanse of future, time's apportionment
> to ordinary mornings, noons, and nights.

All this lay in the world of slender chances
suspended from a filament of breath
severed each second by the blade of danger.
Say you slept a hundred years, then woke
cured but bewildered to an empty world
to take your chances in, with years to spare.
I kiss you. Cured: the word hangs there like smoke.

from **Mirrors of Astonishment** (1992)

ON POETRY

1   Lyric

All possible excrescences lopped off,
its essence must remain
austerely crystalline. True lyric should
exclude all trivia. Thus Critic X

objects to Proust's including
the lift-boy's sister shitting in the back
seats of hired cabs as "mere detail
that must have struck the master as worth quoting

but seems to us obtrusively grotesque."
Poppycock. Proust wasn't writing lyric.
The creel he hauled up groaned with what he both
found and invented, all equally fresh,

slippery, shining with imagination.
The epic gates of ivory and horn
may as well open wide for defecation
as eating, sex, or sleep.

Homer's horizons accommodate heroes
who drink wine, piss on the beach, weep at sundown,
go to bed with braceleted boys or women
and every dawn the sun comes up again.

But lyric's narrow margins
ought to tighten, tighten like a migraine.
Small explosions follow, their throbbing
a welcome price for maimed intensity.

II Trivia

By trivia I mean unmediated
worship of nature; the idolatry
of mere delight in an unfolding iris,
a scudding storm cloud, one's own tenderly

remembered hemorrhoid. The language of
all these must be interpreted. No one
ripening apple cups its simple sense.
Take away the apple, keep the fruit's

lingering odor: regret for past
hours spent on hands and knees in search
of strawberries remains, and is enough.
Red-stained knees, mouths, fingers—these are sweeter

in the recalling than subordinated
to each year's petty facts: arthritic knees,
plague of black flies, or a foraging
toddler who ate the berries faster

(devouring time) than you could ever pick them.
See apples turn to strawberries on this
magic palate. Or a smell of onions
and okra frying in olive oil

conjures up a village's bright mornings.
Whole years fit into a tiny window,
sunny, untouchable, distant,
the scene it frames an idol out of nature.

III Nature

Hardest of all. Is it whatever fails
to stick out, a sore thumb,
from its surroundings, or just what we're used to,
or something no human hand has touched?

"Papa Bear hammers nails into the roof,"
whoever wrote the version my son reads
felt the need to add to "Goldilocks."
Homo Faber twiddles his thumbs for want

of natural work. Nature as order asks
constant attention; nature as wildness, neglect.
Though Wesley Ward's junked cars offend my sense
of order and of nature, year by year

they're masked by higher grass and growing trees,
will vanish soon (I hope) like Ozymandias . . .
The books piled on my table
are also unnatural, messy, hard to dispose of

in their small way. Itself a pied creation,
poetry explores a middle ground,
one foot stuck in a rusty pick-up truck,
one hand shading the eyes against

sun, moon, stars—whatever natural light
we see our earthly lives in.
Not one but two lights, and a single urgent
finger pointing—is it up or down?

CITY AND COUNTRY

1 The Retreat

Ah, the conspiratorial
ganglia of this city,
its macedoine of clues,
its plethora of uses.

Why did the barber smile
when J. and I passed by fighting?
Why does the vegetable lady
have a blue bruise over her lip?

Must every passer-by,
must every casual spy,
every sentient eye
you happen to encounter

embody something huge as history?
Overwhelmed by data,
we punctually scuttle
each summer to the country

or seashore's blessed blankness.
Portentous tigers may
stalk the dusty garden,
may pace the stony beach,

but they do not accost us.
They hardly seem to see us.
No mirroring accusing
eyes peer from trees or water.

Our reflections here
have to be self-sufficient.
Or you could say we leave
to see the city and to be unseen.

ii The Dream of Divesting

When it's finally time to go away,
how much of myself shall I shed?
Happy the empty suitcase;
happier the empty head.

Deliciously divested,
I open the door of the house
only to find what was a farm
is now a grandiose

opera hall. Rehearsing
"*La ci darem,*" I wear
nothing but sheer soprano;
the rest is all thin air.

The summer dream of stripping
has come true, then? Not yet.
These are the words I'm singing
in the dream duet:

Take off my nightgown,
let my hair fall down,
put a crown of stars upon me;
wrap me in myth,
let desire with
its purple fire clothe me.

Absolute nudity
is a deluded hope.
The very air I'm singing
is woven trope on trope,

a tissue of rich figures
we are condemned to wear
as long as we're condemned
to breathe the air

of city or of country.
Forever greener grass
is cleverly reflected
in memory's glass.

III   At a Distance

We eat our daily bread but we don't taste it.
Familiarity doesn't breed contempt;
it fosters an invisibility

so thorough that to remember anything
we have to have recourse to elegy.
Take this June in the country.

Lilacs, fireplace, barn,
meadow, rainbow, anniversary—
all tempered with nostalgia's deepest green.

Our crude attention happily responds
to what is unintelligible still,
utterly new and strange as an infant's squall.

Tirelessly then we work to recreate
the primal moment, building little shrines
tagged for convenient reference:

"This we did here, remember?"
I do remember. Generous attempts
doomed because they're hopelessly belated.

The magic has leaked out of the foundation.
The imitation bed's made up, the table
spread, the lilacs faithfully perform.

We see the season, eat and sleep and dream.
In the city we dream of the country.
In the country we dream of a country

always anterior and always distant.
Distance is the only magic key.
Distance is the aphrodisiac.

Except for the golden child asleep between us,
everything—including you and me—
looks better at a distance.

This is being written in the country.

EXPRESSION

Our faces peeled to raw banality
        of flesh and bone
seem to say nothing looked at one by one,
convey so little that we gladly don
        cheeks, lips. The mask of flesh
fits each soul's uniqueness with a face
molded by selfhood to expression.

I used to be so certain! From the skull
issued an inimitable voice
        singing its quintessential
        tune. And each eye's shade
of green, gray, brown was like a forest glade
        whose pine or maple tree
was captured by, reflected in the soul
        as colors are laid on

by a skilled painter. Physiognomy
        in every architectural
        flourish and least detail
I knew was eloquent of the ineffable
inner stuff—call it spirit, self, or soul.
Words are debased coinage; pass them by.
Gauge a person by a flashing eye,
        a lip's significant curl.

Because we none of us possess a mirror,
        I stubbornly persisted
        in this romantic error,
aspiring to interpret self from skin,
until a snapshot rudely showed me the
        extent to which the soul,
immune to wishes, to idolatry,
        remains illegible.

Mother and toddler ride a carousel.
Their faces show no feeling at all.
      Clues to their states of soul
are how she bends; his hands that clutch the pole—
the eloquence of bodies poised in space,
      iconography without a face
because our human masks are far too thick to show
      glimmerings of selves we barely know.

IN THE MIDDLE

The story of summer is always somehow the story of sleep,
of covering our heads for the sheer pleasure of oblivion,
and the possibility of peeking out.
Why do you want to know about the past?
the sphinx demanded, crossing muscular arms
over her breasts. *What good will it do to know*
exactly why or how your father died?
Yet a child is supposed to answer the elders' questions,
no matter how bloody his two skinned knees,
brimful of grief his heart, raspberries filling his mouth.
Whose child are you? How did you get to the island?
I don't suppose you walked here on the sea.
Intricate scaffoldings clambered up backwards,
the voyager swings blind through the great hotel.

Brilliant mornings we pull the covers up,
shut out the sun the better to perceive him.
Radiant, he tiptoes in.
The shade pulls shaped like tiny lobster buoys
he tugs, lets light into the dreaming room,
then dives into the middle of the bed
and lies between us, waiting to be born.
I remember my father's warm left and my mother's warm right
thigh as I sat between them on some front seat,
sensing myself even then in a not so permanent
crack of creation I would never stop
issuing from, but the place itself was mortal.
Why do you want to know about the past?

A COPY OF **ARIEL**

Not only is the bookmark still in "Poppies in July,"
but I can smell the mildew still—a seamold's
rich and acrid pale-brown sour tang.
Or is it that the book enfolds a world
bleary but flowering with possibilities?
Each morning I gazed at the milky sea
and it was always morning. It was morning
when, making one more effort to efface
the person I had always been, I thought
"Why not translate 'Poppies in July'
into Greek?" And it was also morning
when my first original Greek poem
was born of gazing. But Plath's poppies first.
I recall those little bloodied skirts,
the thin as paper dry and bloodied lips,
translucent delicacies, onion skins,
and the skeptical question *"Do* you do no harm?"
(my italics) which could be translated
rather than answered.

        As for my own poem,
it never got beyond the first two lines:
Phortoma gaidouria kai karpouza!
Phtasane ta kaikia ap'ta nisa.
("Cargo of donkeys and watermelons!
The fishing boats have arrived from the islands.")

The poem was no more than a transparent
container for four juicy neuter plurals
(donkeys, watermelons, caiques, islands)—
an embryonic grammar beyond which
I failed to move. I had no more to say.
No human face looked back at me. A life,
motives—illegible. What I still can see
is the horizon, pallid amulet
beckoning above the shimmer of gray sea;

and sense, even now, my dim determination
to hold onto what could in any case
never be lost. So that those ghostly poppies
and smell of paper mildewing in mist—
smell edible, perishable as meat—
both open vistas, far, symmetrical;
whereas the donkeys (hoisted with a crane
onto the old *limani*) or the glistening
bulbous melons bouncing in the hull,
naked of meaning but for brilliant outlines,
were called back into being only through
the rules of grammar and my meager Greek
word hoard—called back, though, as genuine
visions, even if the haze through which they shone
yielded to each morning's arrow: sun.

LEARNING TO TALK

Some of the ways my parents passed me language
or I just took it: Mother's groaning platter
of pristine etymologies
glossily displayed and known by heart
somehow without ever being sullied;
Grandfather's journal during his engagement
("Showed B. my sonnet. She asked why it only
had fourteen lines"); my father's putative
unfinished novel of the Occupation
in Athens (lost? or merely from the first
a dreamwork?); my elder sister's private
diary secretly filched and read
by the same reprehensible young person
whose son at not quite three corrected her,
me, I mean, fussily, for calling something
red when it was "actually orange."

None of us was afraid to put a name
to anything; but neither did we lift
our faces from the pages of our books.
And our insinuating pedantry,
nibbling at an utterance's edge,
still adheres: the way we picked up words,
more or less gently licked them into shape
like Vergil's verses, sent them gingerly
out into the great world.
Periphrases, lacunae, and corrections;
the cunning madman's fixed hyperbole;
the squishy diction of gentility—
what talents, what avoidances, what losses!

ROADBLOCK

Call me the bee buzzing in the museum.
The younger sister fussing through a house
still stiff with loss.
The meddling goblin in the mausoleum.

My dream: with three in the front seat, we drive
under a bridge- and halt. A huge gray bus
blocks the whole road, including us,
the only travelers who are left alive.

It's drizzling; the windshield wiper blades
busily gesture, yet we're nearly blind.
You two seem not to mind
blank windows, pulled-down shades.

I mind. I want to get out and explore,
to move around
the deathly obstacle. "Don't make a sound,"
you say. (Who are you?) "Don't go near that door."

Our mountain drive last month—that wasn't dreamed.
We three again. We ran a dog down. I
alone looked back, alone let out a cry.
I saw it lying in its blood and screamed.

So tell me what these images portend.
Am I a noisy bird of evil omen
or just a person, apprehensive, human,
moving ahead, kid sister into woman,

stonewalled by death each time she rounds a bend?

GENEALOGIES

The Muses are the daughters of Memory.
Family resemblances flash out at moments
when the reminiscent voice begins
either to crack under the weight of feeling
or to lift off as lyric, winging, soaring
at once toward knowledge and away from facts.
It turns its back on the familiar,
strains after still unformulated questions
if a voice can have a back to turn.
But who can doubt intelligence is bodied?
What's miscalled inspiration merely means
the daughters take dictation from the mystic
mother; fish treasure from a well so empty
that at the bottom gravel gleams like mica,
flickering forms that mock the seeker's eye.

Flickering forms that mock the seeker's eye
and come from where? Jealously Memory
guards her stockpile till the daughters turn
to less demanding tasks, then overwhelms them.
They have no choice; to turn the treasure down
means to lose it. So, obedient
although still abstracted, they remember.
The law of anamnesis reenacted
over and over blurs the boundaries
of learning, inspiration, recollection.
I turned to you, a flower to the sun.
The shadowed face as what to love and also
a way of loving was your legacy.
Later I ventured on a variation:
turning my own dream-heavy head away.

Turning my own dream-heavy head away,
I sped along the parallel and found
solitude in the island of my body.
Mirrors of astonishment, water, trees
spoke through the window of my meditation,
truer than human voices in their weaving
between the phases, inattention giving
way to thirst, or hunger to abundance.
You never taught me how to make a choice,
or make a friend, or how to think of endings.
How to exclude. That choosing means exclusion.
A task I had to come to on my own,
you never taught me how to tell the truth.
Setting things down came second. First you taught me—
slow pupil, I'm still learning—how to read.

Slow pupil, I'm still learning how to read.
Reading is a refinement, a digestion
of those crude texts which in their turn revise
the endless rough drafts of experience.
Unearthing words renews connections where
something had sifted numbly to the bottom,
broken in the trench, the careless diggers
shouldering their shovels, stomping off to lunch.
Some small bridge existed, even so;
hence Auden's Caliban refers to the
restored relation, not the new-created.
Creation's sheer raw heat is what confounds.
The rest is polish, wear and tear, reworking—
all the tasks of recollection's children.
And I am one, and you are recollection.

And I am one, and you are Recollection,
the double parent with whose many lives
I briefly coincided. Brevity
that once was spiked with elegy appears
natural now as shadows passing over
obedient to a law. Obedient
and even calm between impatiences,
I fumble at the rudder, steer my life,

peering for omens in the winking cistern
or turning to the sky. Miasmas rise
steadily from calendar and mirror.
Habit disperses them; they thin like smoke,
there but invisible. Father, I age
and turn to you as I would turn a page.
The Muses are the daughters of Memory.

from **Other Worlds Than This** (1994)

Translations

ADDE MERUM VINOQUE . . .

by Tibullus

Fill up my glass again! The anodyne
for this poor lover's pain is sleep—and wine.
And when I've swilled enough to sink a ship,
no busybody better wake me up.
A cruel door stands between my girl and me,
double-locked with a determined key.

Damn you, door! May rainstorms mildew you,
or well-aimed lightning burn you through and through.
Aren't you moved by all my misery?
Please, door, open just a crack for me,
but carefully—don't creak. If I have said
harsh words, may curses light on my own head.
I hope you've not forgotten all my prayers,
and all the times I hung your knob with flowers.

You, Delia, must be bold and cunning too;
Venus helps those who help themselves, you know.
Whether a boy sneaks to a strange room or
stealthily a girl unlocks a door,
Venus teaches sorties out of bed,
teaches our footsteps soundlessly to pad,
or lovers to communicate by sighs
before the hoodwinked husband's very eyes.
But you must have initiative, and dare
to prowl around at midnight without fear.

Take me—I wander through the streets all night.
Plenty of thieves and muggers are in sight,
but Love protects me from the switchblade knife
scenario ("Your money or your life!").

In holiness a lover's safety lies;
it's needless to envision plots and spies.
No frosty winter night can do me harm;
rain falls in torrents, but I'm safe and warm.
True, now I'm suffering; that could turn around
if Delia beckoned me without a sound.

Whoever sees us, please pretend you didn't!
Venus prefers her lovers snugly hidden.
Don't make a racket, do not ask my name
or blind me with an outthrust torch's flame.
If you were fool enough to see us, then
pray to the gods that you'll forget again.
The tattle-tale must learn the parentage
(tempest and blood) that fuels Venus' rage.

But even if some busybody tells
your husband all about us, magic spells
will seal his eyes. A witch has promised me.
I've seen her pull the stars down from the sky.
Her stars can change a running river's flow,
split open graves and let dead spirits go.
From pyres still smoldering she can wheedle bones,
commanding ghostly troops with weird groans;
then, sprinkling milk, she orders them away.
Clouds she disperses from a sullen sky.
In midsummer she can make it snow;
she knows Medea's herbs and where they grow;
the hounds of Hecate she can tame at will.

To cheat him, she's concocted me a spell
to chant three times and each time spit as well.
From that time on, no matter what he sees,
he'll be unable to believe his eyes.
But keep away from other men! He'll be
suspicious of every man but me.
This sorceress claimed that she could cure me too;
her charms and herbs could set me free—of you.
She purified me at the witching hour
by torchlight, and slew victims with her power.
But what I prayed for was a love to share;
life without you would be bleak and bare.

Iron-headed fool, who had you in his bed
but chose a military life instead!
Let him parade his troops of prisoners forth
and pitch his tent on bloody captured earth.
His armor's silver worked with gold, of course,
so let him preen in it astride his horse.
For myself, let me yoke up my two
oxen and plow, so long as I'm with you.
When we are intertwined in one embrace,
sweet sleep on the bare ground is no disgrace.
Why toss on purple counterpanes, awake
and weeping all night for a lost love's sake?
Down comforters, rich bedspreads cannot bring
sleep, nor can soft water murmuring.

Have I offended with my blasphemy,
Venus, and do I pay the penalty?
Can it be said that I've profaned the shrine,
despoiled the altar of its boughs divine?
If this were true I'd go down on all fours
and plant a kiss upon the temple floor;
kneeling in supplication on the ground,
against the door my wretched head I'd pound.

Whoever finds this laughable—you'll see!
You too will suffer from Love's cruelty.
An oldster thinks a lovelorn youth's a joke,
but soon his wrinkled neck is in the yoke.
He whistles senile ditties to the air
and carefully arranges his white hair,
loiters for hours at his beloved's gate
and buttonholes her servant in the street.
Children pursue him, a malicious flock
who spit in their own bosoms for good luck.

Venus, I've always served you faithfully.
Don't burn your harvest in your rage at me!

BOAZ ASLEEP

by Victor Hugo

Boaz had lain down to sleep, worn out.
All day with other threshers he had toiled,
Then made a bed in his accustomed spot
And slept beside the bushels he had filled.

Owner of fields of barley and of corn,
This man was rich, yet wanted to do right.
The water in his mill ran free from smut;
Nor did hellfire in his smithy burn.

His beard flowed silver as an April stream.
No greed or hatred flourished in his crop.
When he spied some poor gleaners passing, "Stop,"
He'd order. "Leave a few ears out for them."

Pure, far from paths of crookedness he strode,
Both character and garb with candor glowing.
His sacks of grain were fountains overflowing
For every poor wayfarer on the road.

A master and a kinsman kind yet strong,
Careful but generous with his estate,
Boaz drew women's glances—not the young.
Young men are handsome, but old men are great.

Old men move back toward their origin,
Depart from change, approach eternity;
Young men's eyes gleam with fire, as we see,
But with a softer radiance old eyes shine.

☙

So Boaz was asleep among his people.
The millstones looked like ruins of a temple,
The slumbering gleaners looked like sculpture too;
And all this happened very long ago.

Israel was ruled by judges in those days.
Tent-dwelling nomads, people fearfully
Shrank from the giant footprints they could see.
The recent flood had softened earth to ooze.

∾

Sleeping such sleep as Jacob must have had,
Or Judith, Boaz drowsed beneath his bower.
The gate of heaven chanced to be ajar;
A dream crept down and lighted on his head.

And in this dream he saw a mighty oak
Sprung from his loins, up to blue heaven growing;
A race of people climbed it link by link
Like a long chain to where a god was dying

(At its roots, a king was singing). He
wondered in his dream, "How can this be?
My sum of years now far exceeds four-score.
I have no sons, and have a wife no more.

It's many years since she with whom I lay
Has left, O lord, my couch to sleep with Thee;
And we are still entwined like people wed,
She partly living and I partly dead.

Impossible! A people spring from me?
How could I be the father of a son?
Youth is triumphant with each new-fledged dawn,
Each morning bursts from night like victory,

But old men shake like trees when winds are howling.
Widowed and aged, upon me night is falling,
O God! My soul inclines toward the brink,
As thirsty oxen bend their brows to drink."

So spoke Boaz in his sleep to God,
Turning his sleep-drenched eyes toward the sky.
A cedar fails to scent a rose nearby;
He didn't sense a woman near his bed.

⧼

While he was sleeping, Ruth, a Moabite,
Had lain down at the feet of Boaz, breast
Bared, and hoping for some unknown light
When daybreak should awaken in the East.

Boaz had no idea that she was there,
And Ruth had no presentiment of God's will.
Sweetness drifted from the asphodel;
From Galgala soft breezes floated near.

Nuptial, grand, and solemn was the night.
Angels must have flown discreetly through
The darkness; one could barely snatch a sight
Of something wing-shaped, flickering, and blue.

Boaz's soft breathing made a sound
Mingled with brooks that tumble over moss.
This month Nature showed her sweetest face.
Each hilltop with lilies now was crowned.

Ruth was dreaming, Boaz sleeping. Earth
Was black. The distant tinkling of a bell . . .
Enormous goodness down from heaven fell.
At such an hour lions venture forth

To drink. In Ur and Jerimadeth, calm.
Stars enameled all the deep, dark sky.
In the West a slender crescent shone,
And Ruth, not moving, opening half an eye,

Peered through her veils, and asked herself what great
God, what gleaner of eternal heat
Had negligently tossed before he left
His sickle into heaven's starry loft.

VOYAGE TO CYTHERA

by Charles Baudelaire

Free as a bird and joyfully my heart
Soared up among the rigging, in and out;
Under a cloudless sky the ship rolled on
Like an angel drunk with brilliant sun.

"That dark, grim island there—which would that be?"
"Cythera," we're told, "the legendary isle
Old bachelors tell stories of and smile.
There's really not much to it, you can see."

Oh place of many a mystic sacrament!
Archaic Aphrodite's splendid shade
Lingers above your waters like a scent
Infusing spirits with an amorous mood.

Worshipped from of old by every nation,
Myrtle-green isle, where each new bud discloses
Sighs of souls in loving adoration
Breathing like incense from a bed of roses

Or like a dove roo-cooing endlessly . . .
No; Cythera was a poor infertile rock,
A stony desert harrowed by the shriek
Of gulls. And yet there was something to see.

This was no temple deep in flowers and trees
With a young priestess moving to and fro,
Her body heated by a secret glow,
Her robe half-opening to every breeze;

But coasting nearer, close enough to land
To scatter flocks of birds as we passed by,
We saw a tall cypress-shaped thing at hand—
A triple gibbet black against the sky.

Ferocious birds, each perched on its own meal,
Were madly tearing at the thing that hung
And ripened; each, its filthy beak a drill,
Made little bleeding holes to root among.

The eyes were hollowed. Heavy guts cascading
Flowed like water halfway down the thighs;
The torturers, though gorged on these vile joys,
Had also put their beaks to use castrating

The corpse. A pack of dogs beneath its feet,
Their muzzles lifted, whirled and snapped and gnawed;
One bigger beast amidst this jealous lot
Looked like an executioner with his guard.

Oh Cytherean, child of this fair clime,
Silently you suffered these attacks,
Paying the penalty for whatever acts
Of infamy had kept you from a tomb.

Grotesquely dangling, somehow you brought on—
Violent as vomit rising to the chest,
Strong as a river bilious to taste—
A flow of sufferings I'd thought long gone.

Confronted with such dear remembered freight,
Poor devil, now it was my turn to feel
A panther's slavering jaws, a beak's cruel drill—
Once it was my flesh they loved to eat.

The sky was lovely and the sea divine,
But something thick and binding like a shroud
Wrapped my heart in layers of black and blood:
Henceforth this allegory would be mine.

Oh Venus! On your isle what did I see
But my own image on the gallows tree?
Oh God, give me strength to contemplate
My own heart, my own body without hate!

THE SWAN

by Charles Baudelaire

I

Andromache, I think of you! This poor
Rivulet where your fabled sorrows gleam,
This downscale Simois where as of yore
Your widow's tears forever swell the stream

Has watered my green memory as well,
Suddenly, at the Place du Carrousel.
Mercurial as human feelings are,
The shapes of cities alter faster far:

Old Paris is no more. I only see
Huts full of bric-a-brac in my mind's eye,
Barrels heaped up, and columns whose rough stone
Splashes of muddy water have turned green.

Caged animals were on display just there;
And there I saw once in the clear cold dawn
When early workers raise a hurricane
Of blackish dust in the still silent air,

A swan. Out of its cage, it dragged its feet
Along the bone-dry sidewalk; glossy white
Pinions trailed the pebbles in its wake.
Near a dry brook-bed opening its beak,

Skittishly flirting feathers in a bath
Of dust, and heartsick for its native lake,
"Oh, water, rain on me! Oh thunder, break!"
The wretched swan was saying. Fatal myth

Emblazoned like an emblem in the sky—
The tremulous writhing neck, the avid head
Outstretched to tell its troubles straight to God—
Cruel and ironic, still in the mind's eye!

II

Paris changes, not my old distress.
New buildings in construction, scaffoldings,
My memories with their stony heaviness,
Old districts—all are now symbolic things.

Thus before the Louvre even now
The image rises: my great swan, its motions
Dignified, mad as any displaced person's,
Obsessed with endless longing—then of you,

Andromache! No longer sheltered in
Your lost lord's arms, slave of Achilles' son,
You huddle in an ecstasy of grief
To mourn for Hector—Helenus's wife!

I think of a consumptive Negress, gaunt
And haggard, scouring the filthy street
For the lost palm trees of her native haunt,
For Africa behind a wall of sleet.

Of losses that can never be made good,
Never! of people draining a whole gulf
Of grief, yes, suckling Sorrow like a wolf;
Of skinny orphans who like flowers fade!

So in the forest of my mind's exile
An ancient memory blows its horn. The sound
Conjures up sailors shipwrecked on an isle,
And prisoners, victims, others without end!

THE VOICE

by Charles Baudelaire

My cradle stood against the bookcase, Babel
Of murky voices. Novel, science, fable,
Greek dust, and Latin ashes made one stew.
When I was tall as a big folio,
Two voices spoke to me. The first was firm,
Also seductive: "This world's full of charm.
What I can do for you, my boy, is make
Your hunger equal to this endless cake."
The other: "Come to dreamland! Come explore
Beyond the merely possible and known!"
This voice was like a wind along the shore,
A rootless phantom singing on its own
With a caressing, terrifying sound.
I answered "Yes! Sweet voice!" And so began
Whatever you might call it—say my wound
And my fatality. Behind the scenes
Of this enormous stage, in an abyss
Of blackness, I see other worlds than this.
Privileged victim of a clear-eyed fate,
I drag along with serpents at my feet.
And since that time the prophet within me
Loves above all the desert and the sea;
I laugh at funerals and weep at feasts,
And in the sourest wine find some sweet taste.
Many a humdrum fact I call a lie,
And fall in holes through gazing at the sky.
My Voice consoles me: "Keep your mad dreams, far
Fairer than the dreams of wise men are!"

THE SEVEN OLD MEN

by Charles Baudelaire

Here specters pluck at passers-by. Oh teeming
City, huge, mysteriously dreaming
Even in daylight! Strange sap secretly
Flows through each constricted passageway.

One morning I was down in the dark street
Whose houses—the mist lent them extra height—
Looked tall as twin banks of a swollen stream.
As actors' moods can infiltrate a scene,

Vile yellow fog crept all along the ground.
I strained for fortitude, the hero's part,
Striving to banish weakness from my heart,
Trudging the track where lumbering tumbrels groaned.

Abruptly an old man appeared to me
In rags the color of the sodden sky.
Plenty of charity would have come his way
But for the wicked glimmer in his eye,

Jaundiced and evil as if steeped in gall.
At his glance the temperature fell.
His matted beard, as rigid as a sword,
Jutted out as that of Judas would.

His legs were at right angles to his back;
He wasn't bent, but broken altogether.
A final touch was added by his stick
So that he hobbled like a crippled creature

Or Jew on three legs. Through the muddy slush
He waded heavily as if to crush
A layer of dead bodies underfoot
Not out of carelessness but out of hate.

Another one was coming—beard, stick, all—
Specter in each detail identical!
A senile twin had sprung from the same hell.
They marched in tandem toward some secret goal.

Innocent victim of an evil scheme
Or dreadful chance, abashed and horrified,
One by one I counted seven of him!
The sinister old man had multiplied.

Whoever laughs at my anxiety
And doesn't shudder out of sympathy,
Please understand: for all their frailty,
These monsters would live on eternally,

Or so it seemed. Could I have borne to see
An eighth advancing inexorably,
Filthy Phoenix, sire at once and brood?
I turned my back on the whole damned parade.

As fitful drunks with double vision stagger,
I hurried home and locked the door in horror,
Exhausted, sick, confusion in my brain,
Mystery, absurdity my twofold pain.

Vainly my reason tried to take command
Over the tempest howling through my mind.
Abandoned, rudderless, my soul danced free
Over a desolate and shoreless sea.

AURORA

by Paul Valéry

Confusion and gloom,
My versions of repose,
Dissipate as the room
Is touched with dawn's first rose.
Endowed with new control,
I straighten up my soul
And I begin to pray.
Barely emerged from depths
Of sleep, courageous steps
Move toward the light of day.

Hail! I salute you, twin
Similitudes, who each—
Smiling, asleep, akin—
Shine out from common speech
And who salute all these
Sounds like a hive of bees
While tremblingly I hold
Onto the lowest end
And cautiously ascend
A ladder of pure gold.

How dawn's illumination
Awakens drowsy groups,
Enlivening with motion
What slumbered as mere shapes!
Some scintillate, some yawn.
Vague fingers stray along
A comb, mother of pearl,
Just surfacing from dreams,
Whose lazy mistress seems
To link it with this world.

Soulful ideas at play,
I've caught you at it now!
What did you do till day
To fend off your ennui?
They answer: "We're forever
Benign. Our presence never
Has betrayed your house.
Not leaving you alone,
We secret spiders spin
Webs in your dwelling place.

Are you not drunk with joy
To see what we have wrought?
Silk suns unnumbered we
Have woven on your thought.
See how we stretch the weft
Over your gloomy cleft,
And with such simple strands
Catch innocent creation
In our reticulation
Of gently trembling bonds."

Their cobwebs' subtle clinging
I break, and go to find
Oracles for my singing
In the forest of my mind.
The universe decrees
That every soul should seize
The height of its desire,
Heeding the faintest sigh;
Lips parted, even I
Sense shudderings in the air.

My shady vineyards here,
Cradles of every chance—
How many forms appear
Before my dreaming glance!
Each green leaf's offering
Is a refreshing spring.
I drink the soft sound in;
For so much juicy flesh
I have no other wish
Than time to taste again.

I have no fear of thorns!
Waking is hard but good.
These mental whips and scorns
Decree a cautious mood.
No charm can cast its spell
Unless it wounds as well
The charmer who in pain
Acknowledges what scars him.
His blood drawn reassures him
The suffering's his own.

By limpid light caressed,
The pool I now draw near.
Borne up along its breast,
My Hope is bathing there,
Haloed above the mass
Of water, clear as glass.
Its power lets her know
What mystic depths achieve
Union within the wave.
She shudders head to toe.

POMEGRANATES

by Paul Valéry

Oh pomegranates! Seeds
So pack your tough, taut rind
They burst it like a mind
Drunk with discoveries.

The sun that works its will
To bring you to fruition
Softens your hard gold shell
And there begins to spill

Obedient to some power
Bright red through each partition,
Each drop a secret jewel.

The wound's illumination
Allows me to envision
Your secret inmost bower.

SPIROCHAETA PALLIDA

by Konstantine Karyotakis

Beautiful, taken all in all, those scientific books
with blood-red illustrations. After several dubious looks
at these, my friend (another beauty) giggled secretly;
and there was beauty too in what her fleeting lips gave me,

which gently yet persistently came knocking at each head.
We opened up so she could march imperiously in,
Mistress Madness. Once inside, she locked the door again.
Since then our life is like a story strange and old and sad.

Logical thought and feeling now are luxuries, excess.
We give them both away for free to any prudent man,
while holding onto childish snickers, wild impulsiveness.
Whatever is instinctive we've committed to God's hand.

Since all of His creation is a horrid comedy,
the author and producer—his intentions are the best—
has rung the curtain down so that we do not have to see
the dazzling performance lost in dimness, dreams, and mist.

Beautiful, taken all in all, our little purchased friend
that winter twilight long ago when, enigmatically
laughing, she leaned forward for a kiss. And she could see
like a yawning gulf the way it probably would end.

PREVEZA

by Konstantine Karyotakis

Death is the cranes
that bump into the roofs and the black wall;
death is the local dames
who make love peeling onions all the while.

Death is each shabby street
with its resonant, resplendent name,
the olive grove, the sea below spread out,
and death of all the other deaths, the sun.

Death the policeman who so carefully
wraps up and weighs his "insufficient" dinner,
and death the hyacinths on the balcony,
the teacher, nose forever in his paper.

Ah, Prevesa, fortress and garrison!
On Sunday we'll go listen to the band.
I got a savings booklet from the bank.
First deposit: thirty drachmas down.

Strolling slowly up and down the quay,
"Do I exist?" you say. "You're not alive!"
Here comes the steamer, and her flag flies high.
His Excellency the Governor may arrive.

If at least one person in this place
from horror, boredom, and disgust would drop,
silent and solemn, each with a long face,
at the funeral we'd live it up.

CHORUS FROM EURIPIDES'S HELEN

Mother of oars, the sea is your lover.
Phoenician galley, skim swiftly over
the grey-green breakers, wind at your back—
dancing dolphins, daughter of Ocean.
Pull at the oars, sailors, sailors,
over the breakers skimming, skimming,
till Helen can touch her land once more
by the swirling river, again can see
the temple dances and festivals,
and can embrace Hermione,
her virgin daughter whose bridal torch
is still unlit.

Give us wings and we would fly
like a flock of birds over the plains,
leaving Libya's winter rains,
led by their commander's cry
over the desert, keeping pace
with clouds that scurry through the sky,
cleaving a path through the Pleiades,
past Orion's midnight glow.
Cry aloud at the river: Oh,
Menelaus has fought and won!
Menelaus is coming home!

With horse-drawn chariots hurry, come,
Castor and Pollux, Tyndareus's twins,
under the star dome, heaven-dwellers,
come here quickly and save your sister.
Over the ocean's salty swell
and dark blue crests of foam that spill,

come on the wings of heaven's wind
and purge the rumor from every mind,
wipe out that persistent lie
about where lovely Helen lay,
the lie that blames her for the war
although she never went to Troy—
never set foot in Apollo's towered city.

from **The Empty Bed** (1995)

ALTERNATIVES

Our argument went walking down the street.
Fresh light bounced off the water:
a harbor was behind us, out of sight
except for these exuberant refractions,
morning's hope and afternoon's late ripeness

arm in arm. What time was it? Where were we?
I craned for street signs; could decipher nothing.
Radiant, rinsed, the slates beneath our feet
shone up at us, wet silver.
Was this the city where we'd always lived?

SPRING

Here come the new pastels! Magnolias fling
their pink hearts wide, forsythias explode.
Winter's subterranean fires accede
to spring.

If I were in this picture, would it be real?
inquires the child, observing a black border
between the worlds. It garbles sunlit order.
Grass, crocuses conceal

imperfectly an energy that sleeps
through months of cold and every April stirs.
As if on schedule, I hear her curse
the kids whose shouts have woken her. She leaps

from her dank ambuscade,
roused from hibernation by their play
who cower, whisper, giggle, run away.
She shuffles back to the rag bed she's made

under a bench. Next my father's ghost
observes the children seesaw, swing, and climb.
Silent, he calls "Be careful!" What's the time?
Dazzled in gritty sunshine, I have lost

the thread, can only grope at doubleness.
Spring greenery is no
less real for being so
thinly spread. The black beneath the grass

pulls at the children shoving at the sky.
Winter's secret melts. I am restored.
Hard spring light pours down without a word
into the pure, the newly naked eye.

CHIASMUS

We are comparing notes on honesty.
"Only if I love someone can I

summon the guts to speak the truth," I say,
and offer nervously

"I guess that's normal." "On the contrary,
people confide in strangers," you reply.

So that it's to their loved ones that they lie?
is my reaction (uttered silently).

Reading the stifled thought, you glance at me
fondly, wearily, illegibly.

We all are implicated either way,
your muted gaze both says and doesn't say.

BENEFIT NIGHT, NEW YORK CITY BALLET

Once in its mannered mode
the dance appeared to me
a dusty stiff brocade
of faded mystery.

But this was years ago.
Later it came to seem
a vain if gallant blow
aimed at the cruel regime

of time and gravity
by beauty to defy
the merciless decree:
we grow old, sicken, die.

The years that press us down
carve sullen masks of age.
Eyes fixed on the dim ground,
we creep across our stage.

Now sitting here with you
in the enchanted dark
I still hold to this view.
The sweating dancers work

lightly to lift a great
somber collective pall—
mortality's dead weight—
from you and me and all

who, separate, doomed, and dumb,
can drink in nonetheless
our share of the sublime.
The dancers dance for us:

our grief, love, vanity.
Their bodies form a screen
between humanity
and the pull of the unseen.

The burdens we all bear,
great or small, find ease
this evening in the sheer
radiance of disguise.

For as we raptly gaze
at limbs in cool blue light
sculpting a carnal maze
of intricate delight,

of passions sketched on air,
it is ourselves we see,
divested of despair.
You turn and smile at me.

THE LAST MOVIE

In memory of Charles Barber

Saturday, April 5. Welles's *Othello*:
black and white grid of rage,

steam of sheer fury spewing from the vent
of violence that followed where they went.

Wind howled on the battlements, but sun
gilded glum canals. The lovers floated

beneath black bridges, coupled in stone rooms.
The unrepentant villain (at the start

so all the rest was flashback)
dangled from a cage

squinting inscrutably at the funeral
procession winding through the town below.

The air was full of wailing.
Knives of sunlight glittered on the sea.

We lurched out onto Fifty-Seventh Street.
You said "I think I'm dying."

Next week your eyes went out.
Shining under the lamp,

your blue gaze, now opaque,
your face drawn sharper but still beautiful:

from this extremity you can attempt
to rise to rage and grief. Or you can yield

to the cozy quicksand of the bed.
You wave your hand at walls of books:

"What do I do? Do I throw all these away?"
Their anecdotes, their comforts—now black glass.

THE WOLF IN THE BED

From when you still could see,
do you remember the print beside your bed?
Doré's "Red Riding Hood":
the wide-eyed little girl
shares a pillow with the bonneted
beast. Recall the sidelong
look that links the child
and the shaggy monster
snuggling beside her.
Blankets pulled to their chins
conceal the tangled matters underneath:
a secret region, shadowy deep forest
through which a covered basket
is being carried, bread and wine
and books to the sick one's bedside.
You are the girl in bed beside the beast
or you're the grandmother, I visit you—
but no, since it's my mother, too, who's dying.
Is she in bed with you, since both are breathed on,
crowded, jostled by the restless wolf?
Now I arrive and climb in with you both
(the wolf makes room for me a little while)
and gingerly, so as not
to jar your various lifelines,
cradle you in my arms, my friend, my mother,
and read you stories of children
walking unattended through dark woods.

UPON MY MOTHER'S DEATH

In memory of Elizabeth C. Hadas

The empty bed. And instantly I knew
and also didn't, as I do
and do not even now

where she had gone
precipitously, leaving me alone
to telephone

and do whatever else had to be done.
First, for example, furnish my ID
lest some impostor claiming to be me

should grab her few belongings; next, take them
in long sealed boxes home (but now whose home?);
and last myself continue to become

her who was gone.
This gradual process had been going on
for all our two lives' simultaneous span

but now I lifted her
once chunky person, feather-
light abruptly now, henceforth, forever,

ferried her backward from the empty bed.
Where? Anywhere instead
of that pristine dominion of the dead,

straight to the corridor
where chatting nurses eyed a visitor:
would this belated daughter shed a tear?

No. Yes. No. Yes. Then I absorbed the sense,
the respite, brief and sweet, the recompense:
living, to love the quick and dead at once.

Deciphering this later, I read "lose"
for "love"—a logic I dare not refuse.
Love lorn live lose lone—need we really choose?

As when I wrote of C. "Your absence walks"
but later read it as "Your absence works";
both ways mean a blurry sleeper wakes.

Again, C., dying, left some books to me—
or was it "lent" them? Generosity
either way you read it—legacy

stretching across the boundaries of love,
defying the short time we're let to live,
the scanty sum it's possible to give.

Only for grief is our capacity
limitless. Illegibility
has a silver lining, I now see.

It blurs the limits of mortality.

MAY

As soon as the cold old sun gets warm,
a powerful impulse says *Lie down*.
Down on a bench; in the lap of noon;
on the green bosom of a lawn;
down on a hillside, under a tree,
in mother's absence. In or on,
horizontality's all one.
Effaced each spring a little more
by being forty-two, three, four,
wrapped in invisibility,
I lie and look across the sky.
Near the horizon a streak of green
swells like a harbinger of dawn—
not green like new leaves everywhere,
rather a verdant atmosphere.
I tilt my face, luxuriate—
chin up and eyes shut—in the heat,
warmth that this year feels different.
Spring means all it ever meant,
but the earth where I lay my head
covers my two beloved dead.
They do not say "Forsake the sun."
They say "We loved it, and we're gone."
That golden magnanimity!
Ten minutes is enough for me.
Opening my eyes, I readjust
mind and body. For I must
gradually as in a dream
return to vertical again,
stand up and somehow move beyond
my buried mother, my buried friend.

RECOVERIES

Sweet Briar, Virginia, November 1992; Alsace, pre-1924

A college pool, central Virginia.
The octogenarian who swims next to me
for half an hour at noon each Saturday
recalls Olivier's confiserie,
the best in Strasbourg when he was a boy.
Et ceci se passait dans des temps très anciens,
is what I'm briefly tempted to reply,
having been translating Victor Hugo
today. "This happened very long ago."
I smile and nod and kick and swim away.
Delicious smells and tastes accompany
me along the warm blue shimmering lane.
Cream and butter, chocolate, raspberry . . .
Can such rich pastries ever be again?

460 Riverside Drive? No time

The old apartment's empty, dingy, brown,
Riverside cum West End cum nursing home.
Dressed in khakis, weary, old, and slow,
my long absent father's back in town.
He and I meet by appointment here
to go through papers? Books? It isn't clear.
We want to chat, but we've forgotten how,
so many years have passed with him away.
And time is running out. Tomorrow we
must go our separate ways forever. Oh,
I babble, let me go and buy some snacks—
horseradish, kippered herrings, bagels, lox . . .
I try to think what other foods we shared.
He tries to smile at me. He strokes his beard.
Without a word, we both have taken in
we'll never have a place to live again.

The acrid desolation of the dream
is tangy as a herring packed in cream.

Greenwich Village, mid-1950's

Once upon a time near Union Square,
but I will never know exactly where,
high in a loft recorders used to rest
carefully sheltered in a tall fur nest.
These recorders' pale red-headed owner
taught recorder to my elder sister.
My new friend, a painter, knew this teacher
because she studied Plato with her lover.
For this recorder teacher had a lover—
an actress and a Holocaust survivor.
and a Greek scholar, and a scholar's daughter.
I was the little sister. I remember
standing shyly waiting in the foyer
studying the wood of each recorder,
soprano, alto, bass. Mouthpiece of amber?
Blond wood or dark? The fur (wolf? fox?) was silver.

St. Luke's Hospital, May 20, 1992

Hurrying to the hospital last May,
late in the afternoon, a lovely day,
I slow down slightly to admire the sky.
Mommy is tired; she can wait for me
a few more minutes. Because yesterday
she liked a coconut Italian ice
I bought her on the corner of Broadway,
I buy another. Lemon is my choice.
I walk and lick; she'll finish it. We'll share.
Her illness is not contagious.
I reach her room and nobody is there.
The bed is empty and my mother gone.
Unnoticed, melting lemon leaves a stain
on my jacket. When I take this in

later, the sequence plays itself again:
the stroll, the sweet, the blankness at the end.
If I could make this melting come undone,
would I have seen my mother one more time?
If I clean my sleeve, do I erase
my final expectation of her face?

23 *Waverly Place, June 1992*

About to ring the bell of a good friend,
I encountered Richard. In his hand
was a plastic box of candied ginger.
He held it toward me with a courteous gesture,
munching meanwhile. Nodding toward the door
of the apartment I was aiming for,
he raised his brows and queried "How much more?"
"Bad," I replied. We didn't speak out loud.
I took the proffered candy, sucked and chewed
its fibrous sharpness. Nothing more to say.
We sketched a wave and then both moved away,
he to the elevator, I the door.
No surprises waited for me there.
I knew beforehand how my friend was lying
disoriented, feeble, blind, and dying.
Each visit was a vigil. So I sat
taking in the candied ginger's heat.

Coda

The future's where we place our hope and fear.
What's done is done. The past cannot recur.
Anecdote, dream, and memory all refer
to experience no longer there.
Yet look at what is rising through the air!
Fox fur, ginger, melting lemon ice
successively appear. Can we live twice?
Is nothing lost? I reach a new conclusion:
leave the future to its own confusion.

My business is with what I find I know
through story, memory, dream. Since this is so,
I am a vessel full beyond the brim
even as life leaks out, a steady stream
of losses running toward oblivion.
But how to make one's daily life maintain
a balance between plenitude and pain,
such fullness and such unremitting waste?
Ginger offered in an outstretched hand.
A blond recorder resting in its stand.
Kippers. Pastries. A remembered taste.

PECULIAR SANCTITY

> . . . the tradition which affirmed the peculiar sanctity of the
> sick, the weak, and the dying . . . perhaps came to an end
> for literature with the death of Milly Theale.
> —Lionel Trilling, "Mansfield Park"

Except it didn't. It went underground
as some diseases have been known to do,
returning with a vengeance in our time.
To note the renaissance of elegy
as the defining genre of our day
is not to claim for form
merely the reflex of a pendulum
stupidly swinging. There are differences.
First of all, a fierce self-righteousness
beats its drum through our diffused distress.
Secondly, people take enormous pride
in giving utterance to grief and loss.
It is as if we shoved huge stones aside
to make room for our little threnodies.
Silence is shameful, more than shameful, death.
Is speech not life, then, animal instinct,
survival's automatic pilot, breath?
No; it requires courage. Thirdly, though
for silence and for speech the penalty
our plague exacts is utterly the same,
we are supposed to rage, seethe, overflow
with fury; brandish, not just grief, but blame,
level reproaches at the government.
How could so many be allowed to die?
Fourthly, it is not correct to say
"I'm dying of"; one says "I'm living with,"
thus adding to the gallantry of myth.

In mortal sickness, courage is no lie.
With or without peculiar sanctity,
people have always managed as they could.
And once the sick one takes the downward road
to that broad region shrouded in twilight,
similarities with those before
become more marked than differences of mode.
The figures look the same: tall Tenderness
bends by the bed to offer a caress.
And everyone who passes or who stays
must grapple with the place's doubleness:
the tremulous wish to live at any price
versus the drawn-out longing for release.
When what the scourge can do is done at last,
the bystanders all having done their best;
when everyone's acknowledged this to be
something not curable by elegy
(silence is death, and so is poetry),
they rise, go out, and seek the light of day
for a little while. They turn away,
yes, but only for a breathing space
from the new, old, peculiar sanctity,
before returning to their grisly task.

THE HINGE

Resentments of grown children: slanting, thin,
grudging like a peevish autumn rain.
Reproaches we all visit on our parents.
The teller on the couch
reeling out old grievances
with practiced fluency is less resentful
than the upstanding orphan resolutely
refusing to find fault
with the unforgivable
death of his mother. Listen.

Wordsworth writes of his mother at a slant,
rather refers than mourns. Thus: "Early died
My honoured Mother, she who was the heart
And hinge of all our learnings and our loves."
Warm beating center, then, and also that
which folds so things pass through. The son continues:
"She left us destitute, and, as we might,
Trooping together." Beggars on the road?
Brood of the mother hen mentioned a few lines back?
And where in all this is the father? Absence
shadows the story. "Little suits it me
To break upon the sabbath of her rest
With any thought that looks at others' blame."
Who are those others? Wordsworth shakes his head,
discouraging conjecture as he opens
the door a hair's breadth further to admit
a crack of light. For, his lips pursed, he adds:
"Nor would I praise her but in perfect love.
Hence am I checked." Yet he goes on from there
"In gratitude, and for the sake of truth,
Unheard by her," to thoughts akin to thanks.
Correcting what ghost voices?
Answering what reproaches? Made by whom?

Then Henry James upon his mother's death
when he was thirty-nine: "She was our life.
She was the house, the keystone of the arch.
She held us all together, and without her
we are scattered reeds." Not destitute,
trooping together—this time strewn apart.

Whether of straggling children or sad adults,
the legacy is desolation. Whether
our mothers and our fathers live or die,
but more especially when they die, the sin
is unforgivable. I blame the one
for dying too soon, leaving a poor troop.
I blame her in the sabbath of her rest,
deaf to her son's periphrases, resentments.
I blame the absent father for his absence
if he was absent—worse if he was present.
I blame the other mother, full of years,
for letting slip the keystone of the arch.
And when we're done with blame, reproach, resentment,
the creaky hinges of the heart can open.
In the artists' colony, it's winter.
A writer's mother sends from California
boxes of scarves for all her daughter's colleagues.
A father sends a box of Clementines.
My mother sends me out into the snow
in silence where I listen for her voice.

SONG

Even if every summer past were calling,
    fingers of recognition at the stretch
       waving through cloud,
how much more delight could be allowed?
    How far can gesture reach
       when every moment you are falling, falling?

The mode is elegy
    in whose red light somehow you walk
       forward and also
glance backward as you go.
    When friends bend near to comfort you with talk,
       is it inevitable that they lie?

Not that I could remember or defend
    just why I love you. Possibly
       the way that we refuse to sacrifice
the rendezvous of eyes,
    or that with sudden snorts of laughter we
       puncture the pompous zero of an end.

ARGUMENTS OF SILENCE

> Do you wish people to think
> well of you? Don't speak.
> —Pascal

> Silence = death.

I

Silence as friend. For what can grow without it?
As enemy. For we know what it is said to equal.

If silence equals death, does death equal silence?
Necessary condition, not sufficient.

Only in the charged silence after death
are certain voices heard, while the chat of the living

dwindles behind an invisible veil or glaze
or curtain that may rise to further speech.

II

Silence as style, as stubbornness, as stoical
courage, expedience, patience. Or as fear.

"There's nothing more to say," and walked away.
But how do I know what's there until I say it?

The impulse swells, as fountains do not stop,
as pressure building causes corks to pop:

new takes, new combinations. Or not new
but as my lips interpret an old law.

III

I salute you, friends who would not button
your lips, but kept them, chapped and bloody, open;

who refused to huddle caged as in contagion,
forced to find your balance from between

the horns of the dilemma how to live
at once outside and inside of your bodies

and dance and balance not struck dumb by fear,
your voice a thread, clue to what labyrinth?

IV

That certain words are tinny in our time
(*recovery community denial*

culture diversity even maybe *silence*
even dare I breathe it sometimes *death*);

that speech is not always heroic, not
always interesting or necessary;

that silence is as likely to mean sleep,
exhaustion, or discretion, as death

doesn't release us from the snare of language.
True, wives and husbands, children and their parents

know without speaking what is wished or meant—
the curse of family life, and the reward.

Habit, telepathy, passion:
nothing exempts us from our chatty birthright.

The danger's hardly tyranny by silence.
It's hard to shut us up while we draw breath.

If anything can guarantee our silence,
death can. But silence doesn't equal death.

LULLABY II

As if there were no enemy,
evening rocks me into sleep.
Tomorrow's possibility
undoes the bodice, lets me breathe
out, in evenly. A deep
valedictory sobbing breath
commemorates a span of time
gone as if it had never been.
Yes, we bravely resist the new.
But sun, moon, the beloved's name
we exile to oblivion
and do not speak of all we know.

Histories of ups and downs,
of arguments and stillnesses
cast shadows on the wall of days
silence envelops here, as snow
sifting into a hollow place
erases what was there to see.
Memory rising in the eyes
peaks to knowledge and subsides,
leaving a wash of images
stranded like seaweed at low tide.
We recognize this dear debris
and do not look for all we know.

MARS AND VENUS

(Botticelli, ca. 1475)

Gold tape gently billowing with her breathing,
triple V's at bosom and sleeve and ankle
point to partings, leading the eye to where her
                              body emerges.

Wait: this painting is an enormous V-ness.
Look how unemphatically, almost absent-
ly her left hand seems to be plucking one more
                              labial gilded

entry between her waist and her knee. Reclining,
she becomes a series of languid valleys
who herself creates an entire other
                              landscape of V-ness

in her consort. Slumbering, numb, the war-god—
head thrown back; neck, shoulders, torso open—
seems oblivious equally to the lady
                              and to the satyrs,

naughty toddlers, trying on Mars's helmet,
blowing conches into his ear, or crawling
gleefully through his corselet, their behavior
                              an awful nuisance

all for nothing. Here in this vague green valley
lamb and lion, love and war are united
by indifference equally to these babies
                              and to each other.

Do the little faunlets call Mars their Daddy?
Either way, his answer is not forthcoming.
Drained by amorous combat, the god is elsewhere.
                              Vigilant Venus

gazes, not at him, nor at us, but rather
seems the merest eyeflick away from over-
seeing Sandro putting the final touches
                              onto his family

portrait: Mars and Venus, it's called. Or Father
sleeps while Mother's keeping a watchful eye out
not on the children (are these the couple's children?)
                              but beyond; elsewhere.

Violence sleeps. Desire is in need of further
sustenance: her V's are unfilled, her fingers
seem to press, to promise, half hiding, showing
                              translucent treasures

he has seen and savored to satiation.
Rhyming, secret, intimate, and familiar,
their two mysteries mingle in this: deferral
                              of ever after.

FOUR LIVES, STIRRING

Lemons on damask (one).
Curve of a gold-framed mirror
reflecting blackness. Also black, a squat
empty vase, or maybe bowler hat.
Drained seltzer siphon; shallow teacup (two).
Oblong cake tin. Furled fan.
Enamel coffee pot with pinks, carnations.
Pink-lipped conch brimful of filtered sun.
Lavender linen tablecloth a woman
stretches her arm along
(three) and lays her cheek
against her flowered sleeve
while massive fronds and beanstalk stems of green
climb the far wall. Two women
face each other (four)
across an empty table white as milk
(marble? formica?) lit by a square of window.
No, they are not quite facing one another.
The one in the green turban,
on the far side of the table, faces us
but sits a little skewed from her companion,
as if to shrug off
a relentless gaze, probe, accusation—
that back turned toward us, we will never know.

Surfaces, decorations, interruptions.
Starched white damask. Smell of lemons. Coffee
and wine displaced by cut
flowers in decanter, pot. A drowsy hour
at noon. A downy cheek.

Tulips keep their red or yellow glossy
under a mantle of snow.
Daffodils poke gallantly from sleet.
Under the flowers, vegetables, and fruit
offering their faces to the day
is secret cold, a hidden core of white
concealing in its turn the warm black blanket
that under the eye-aching
brilliance of March shrouds everything that might,
that will strain towards the light.

THE RED HOUSE

Malevich painted you. Can I come in?
I'm on the outside, floating in the void,
trying to name what curdles (milk? wheat? cloud?)

and laps at your foundation like foam.
You have three small white chimneys but not one
window, unless your windows face the sea,

if that is sea there. Lighthouse; tower; friend
planted precisely where the black horizon
unrolls its ribbon under pasty sky,

I wished to settle all
accounts and shut the book.
No, reach and never turn the final page

where—sturdy, poker faced,
sunset-stained to russet—you were standing.
I had walked toward you through a wolfish wood.

I had swum a shark-infested sea
to reach you at that edge
where human constructs dwindle to a verge

and questions like who made you,
responsive to what vision, when and why,
evaporate to mere biography.

But on that day
when my lips and hands stop skittering
and they can scoop my version of the good

out of its hidden niche behind my eyes,
I hope you, tall old house, are what they see,
silent sentry at extremity,

facing the uneasy elements,
your eyes, your windows shrouded with salt spray
or windowless but still awash with light.